Teradata 12 SQL

An Authorized Teradata Certified Professional Program Study Guide

Exam TE0-122

First Edition

ISBN 978-0-9830242-1-7
Printed by Cerulium Corporation

Stephen Wilmes
David Glenday

Copyright

Trademarks

Special Acknowledgement

A special thank you to the following individuals that contributed to the Study Guide content: Barbara Christjohn, Paul Derouin, Susan Hahn, Greg Hamilton, David Micheletto, Rao Nuthakki, Larry Rex, Eric Rivard, and Alison Torres.

About the Author - Steve Wilmes

Steve Wilmes founded Cerulium Corporation in 2007. As Chief Executive Officer, his goal is to establish Cerulium as a premier data warehousing Technology Company. Cerulium's strategic growth is globally focused on six lines of business including education, consulting, BI solutions, productivity tools, application integration and assessment services. These lines of business have been highly successful by utilizing strategic data warehousing solutions provided by Teradata that spans across the consumer, and commercial markets.

Mr. Wilmes has over 20 years of experience in the computer industry and is known to be a detail oriented, results-focused leader. He is an internationally recognized expert in several aspects of data warehousing including hardware, software, SQL, operating systems, implementation, data integration, database administration, and BI solutions.

Mr. Wilmes earned a bachelor's degree in business administration and economics in 1994 from Augsburg College and he is also a Teradata Certified Master.

Mr. Wilmes resides just outside of Columbia, South Carolina, with his wife, Becky. He has been involved with numerous civic, educational, and business organizations throughout his career. Some of his more recent associations include working with the Richland County Sheriff's Department – Region 4 Community Member, and volunteer for local organizations where he shares his technical expertise.

About the Author - David Glenday

David Glenday has 10 years' Teradata consulting experience in the Entertainment, Semiconductor and Telecommunication industries, specifically in the following lines of business: Finance, Strategic Planning, Product Development, Marketing, and Sales.

Mr. Glenday leveraged his business experience, formal education and extensive Teradata knowledge to develop numerous reporting solutions. Solutions include developing and optimizing queries, creating ETL processes and reports using Microsoft Excel and BI tools. He has extensive knowledge integrating web analytic data into Teradata.

Mr. Glenday graduated with a BA in International Business in 1991 and received an MBA in 1997 from California State University Fullerton. He is a Teradata Certified Master.

Mr. Glenday is based outside of Las Vegas, Nevada. He, his wife Kristi and their two children are very active with Cub Scouts, Girl Scouts and his family finds volunteer work very rewarding. David enjoys flying. He received his commercial pilots' license in 1989 and is always looking for more time to devote to this hobby.

Table of Contents

Teradata 12 Certification Study Guide

Chapter 1: The Teradata Certified Professional Program

Enhance your knowledge and career

The Teradata Certified Professional Program (TCPP), launched in 1999, develops and manages Teradata's premier, and only, certification testing program. Teradata authorized training and proctored exams, available globally to customers, partners, and associates are instrumental in establishing an industry-standard measure of technical competence for IT professionals using Teradata technology. Recognized and valued by major global companies using Teradata, more than 51,000 Teradata Certifications have been awarded.

The new Teradata 12 Certification Track consists of seven exams that combine for achievement of six certifications and provides a logical progression for specific job roles. Starting with the core Teradata 12 Certified Professional credential, individuals have an opportunity to demonstrate knowledge by achieving Certification as a Technical Specialist, Database Administrator, Solutions Developer, Enterprise Architect, and the most prestigious Teradata Certification – Teradata 12 Certified Master.

The purpose of this Certification Exam Study Guide is to assist you in your goal of becoming Teradata Certified. The Guide will provide focused content areas, high level explanations around the key areas of focus, and help you to determine areas of further study prior to sitting for the Teradata Certification examination.

The Exam Study Guide will assist you in your Exam preparation, but you must be knowledgeable of the subject areas in order to pass the exam. This Guide is intended for individuals who have completed the recommended training and have the recommended amount of

Teradata experience. We do not guarantee that you will pass the exam simply by reading the Exam Study Guide. Only hard work, hands-on experience, and a positive attitude will help you to achieve exam success. We wish you the very best of luck!

> *"The certification process promoted a systematic learning opportunity on a broad spectrum of topics. This enabled me to apply changes at work that never would have been done otherwise."*
> *– Teradata Certified Master, Blue Cross Blue Shield of NC*

The flowchart and matrix below are designed to help you define a path to the knowledge, skills, and experience needed to achieve Teradata 12 Certifications.

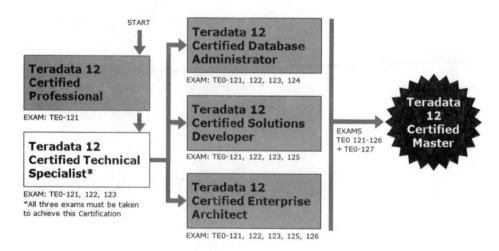

Teradata 12 Certifications

Teradata 12 Certified Professional

Exams Required:

- TE0-121 – Teradata 12 Basics

Must be passed before continuing on certification path

Recommended Teradata Experience:

6-12 months

Recommended Preparation Courses:

- Introduction to the Teradata Database

Teradata 12 Certified Technical Specialist

Exams Required:

- TE0-121 – Teradata 12 Basics
- TE0-122 – Teradata 12 SQL
- TE0-123 – Teradata 12 Physical Design and Implementation

3 Exams to be passed in sequential order

Recommended Teradata Experience:

1-2 years

Recommended Preparation Courses:

- Introduction to the Teradata Database
- Teradata SQL
- Advanced Teradata SQL
- Physical Database Design
- Physical Database Tuning

Teradata 12 Certified Database Administrator

Exams Required:

- TE0-121 – Teradata 12 Basics
- TE0-122 – Teradata 12 SQL
- TE0-123 – Teradata 12 Physical Design and Implementation

Recommended Teradata Experience:

2-3 years

Recommended Preparation Courses:

• TE0-124 – Teradata 12 Database Administration 4 Exams to be passed in sequential order	• Introduction to the Teradata Database • Teradata SQL • Advanced Teradata SQL • Physical Database Design • Physical Database Tuning • Teradata Application Utilities • Teradata Warehouse Management • Teradata Warehouse Administration

Teradata 12 Certified Solutions Developer

Exams Required: • TE0-121 – Teradata 12 Basics • TE0-122 – Teradata 12 SQL • TE0-123 – Teradata 12 Physical Design and Implementation • TE0-125 – Teradata 12 Solutions Development 4 Exams to be passed in sequential order	Recommended Teradata Experience: 2-3 years Recommended Preparation Courses: • Introduction to the Teradata Database • Teradata SQL • Advanced Teradata SQL • Physical Database Design • Physical Database Tuning • Teradata Application Utilities • Teradata Application Design and Development

Teradata 12 Certified Enterprise Architect

Exams Required: • TE0-121 – Teradata 12 Basics • TE0-122 – Teradata 12 SQL • TE0-123 – Teradata 12 Physical Design and Implementation • TE0-125 – Teradata 12 Solutions Development • TE0-126 – Teradata 12 Enterprise	Recommended Teradata Experience: 2-3 years Recommended Preparation Courses: • Introduction to the Teradata Database • Teradata SQL • Advanced Teradata SQL • Physical Database Design

Architecture 5 Exams to be passed in sequential order	• Physical Database Tuning • Teradata Application Utilities • Teradata Warehouse Management • Teradata Warehouse Administration • Teradata Application Design and Development

Teradata 12 Certified Master*

Exams Required:

• TE0-121 - TE0-126: Successful completion of all exams and certifications **PLUS:**
• TE0-127 – Teradata 12 Comprehensive Mastery

7 Exams to be passed in sequential order

*Path for V2R5 Certified Masters (only)

• TE0-12Q: Teradata 12 Qualifying Exam for V2R5

PLUS:
• TE0-127 – Teradata 12 Comprehensive Mastery

Recommended Teradata Experience:

A minimum 5 years practical hands-on experience is highly recommended

Recommended Preparation Courses:

Taking all courses recommended for the Teradata 12 job role certifications:
• Introduction to the Teradata Database
• Teradata SQL
• Advanced Teradata SQL
• Physical Database Design
• Physical Database Tuning
• Teradata Application Utilities
• Teradata Warehouse Management
• Teradata Warehouse Administration
• Teradata Application Design and Development

Certification... Knowledge Building to Mastery

In today's economy, many companies are investing in the training and validation of employees' expertise and knowledge. Teradata's Certification process helps meet these discerning demands in the global market. Teradata has developed a new generation of certification exams and requirements that bring premium value to Teradata 12 Certification credentials.

Top 10 "What's new about the Teradata 12 Certification Track?"

1. Seven exams with all new content based on Teradata Database 12.0.
2. More rigorous certification criteria including a combination of training, study, and practical, hands-on experience.
3. Six new certifications require passing a combination of exams in sequential order starting with the Teradata 12 Basics exam.
4. Five Teradata 12 Certifications must first be achieved to gain eligibility for Teradata 12 Certified Master status.
5. A new Teradata 12 Comprehensive Mastery Exam, among other requirements, has been added to create a more rigorous Teradata 12 Master Certification track.
6. New IP security measures are in place to protect the integrity of exams and certifications.
7. Independent exam scoring procedure provides electronic Results Reports outside of the testing center.
8. Freshly designed certificates and logos available electronically.
9. New state of the art Certification Tracking System manages certification records, fulfillment, transcripts, and credentials validation.
10. The Teradata Certified Professional Program is well established with an experienced team available to support your successful Teradata Certification journey.

Path to Teradata 12 Mastery

A Teradata Certified Master enjoys a distinct advantage in the global marketplace. Employers seek Teradata Certified staff with verifiable knowledge and skills that support their business-critical Teradata systems. The TCPP Certification process helps those individuals who want to deepen their knowledge and build their skills to the highest level.

The path to achieve Teradata 12 Certified Master status is summarized in the matrix below.

If You Are...	Exams Required for Teradata 12 Master Certification
Starting on the Teradata 12 Certification Track	• TE0-121 – TE0-127 All 7 Exams required
Certified V2R5 Master	• TE0-12Q: Teradata 12 Qualifying Exam for V2R5 Masters • TE0-127: Teradata 12 Comprehensive Mastery Exam Both Exams required

The six core Teradata V2R5 exams were retired on March 31, 2010. Teradata V2R5 Certifications will not expire. However, individual V2R5 exams completed in the V2R5 Certification Track are not transferable to the new Teradata 12 Certification Track.

Exam Registration

All Teradata Certification exams are administered and proctored by authorized Prometric Testing Centers. Schedule exams at any authorized Prometric Testing Center by phone or online. In the US and Canada, you may call 1-877-887-6868. Also, a listing of Prometric telephone numbers is available at: www.prometric.com/Teradata. Some countries do not offer online registration.

Where to Find More Information

Information on all authorized Teradata Certification levels, exams, curriculum maps and recommended training, is supplied by a convenient matrix and links located on the TCPP website: www.Teradata.com/Certification.

Teradata Corporation's official certification exams and credentials are developed, copyrighted, and managed solely by the Teradata Certified Professional Program team. There are no other Teradata authorized exams, certifications, or legitimate credentials in the IT industry. To achieve your training and certification goals, pursue only authorized processes and approved courses of study as outlined on the official TCPP website.

Chapter 2: SELECT Command

Certification Objectives

- ✓ Identify the correct use of comparison operators in logical expressions.
- ✓ Evaluate expressions involving NULLs.
- ✓ Identify the correct use of multiple logical expressions in a conditional expression using AND, OR, NOT.
- ✓ Describe the characteristics of the IN, NOT IN logical predicate.

Before You Begin

You should be familiar with the following terms and concepts.

Terms	Key Concepts
Where Clause	How to use with compound comparisons
Like	Character string evaluations
Derived Columns	Arithmetic operations and column alias
Order By	Sorting data ascending and descending

Structured Query Language

Teradata uses the Teradata Structured Query Language, which runs on the Teradata Database to manage objects, data, and permissions.

SELECT Statement

The most frequently used SQL command is the SELECT statement. Because the SQL language also has INSERT, UPDATE, and DELETE statements, many people think that SELECT means "Read". It is the WHERE clause that controls reading. In the SQL language, SELECT means "return for display or processing."

The following chart shows the basic components of a SELECT statement.

SELECT	column names and/or expressions
FROM	table or view name
WHERE	search condition(s)
ORDER BY	column name(s)

Here is an example of a simple SELECT statement.

```
SELECT  *
FROM    student_table
WHERE   class_cd = 'FR'
ORDER BY last_name;
```

Figure 2.1

Note: Every SQL statement must end with a semicolon.

Derived Columns

Frequently, the data residing in a table needs to be changed for display or reporting purposes. A derived column is created when a column in a SELECT performs a calculation.

The following example demonstrates displaying the annual salary amount of employees as a monthly salary amount.

```
SELECT  salary
        ,salary/12
FROM  employee_table;

Result: 9 rows returned

    Salary    (Salary/12)
----------   -----------
  32800.50       2733.38
  48800.00       4066.67
  64300.00       5358.33
  54590.00       4549.17
  48850.00       4070.83
  54590.00       4549.17
  35000.00       2916.67
  42788.88       3565.74
  40200.00       3350.00
```

Figure 2.2

Note: The derived column name defaults to the expression.

Alias Column Names

In the previous example (Figure 2.2), the derived column name defaulted to the expression (salary/12). Though this might be acceptable in some cases, it isn't user-friendly.

To give an output column a different name, use AS <name> following the expression. This allows you to give user-friendly names to derived columns.

If <name> contains a blank or is a reserved word, put it inside double quotes (").

As shown below, the calculation of the annual salary amount as a weekly salary amount has a different column name.

```
SELECT  salary
        ,salary/52 AS "Weekly Salary"
FROM    employee_table;

Result: 9 rows returned

   Salary   Weekly Salary
----------  -------------
  32800.50         630.78
  48800.00         938.46
  64300.00        1236.54
  54590.00        1049.81
  48850.00         939.42
  54590.00        1049.81
  35000.00         673.08
  42788.88         822.86
  40200.00         773.08
```

Figure 2.3

ORDER BY

Relational theory states that the order of columns and the order of rows in a table are arbitrary. When you perform a query, the system will return the rows in a random manner. To request that rows be returned in some sequence, include an ORDER BY clause.

The ORDER BY clause specifies the column(s) to be used in a sort operation, which is performed on the final result set.

The following example sorts all students by their class code.

```
SELECT     last_name
           ,class_code
FROM       student_table
ORDER BY class_code;

Result: 10 rows returned

Last_name                    Class_code
--------------------         ----------
Johnson                      ?
Garrett                      FR
Kojack                       FR
Lamp                         FR
Rieter                       JR
Bond                         JR
McCann                       SO
McCormick                    SO
Phillips                     SR
Craig                        SR
```

Figure 2.4

Note: ASC (ascending) is the default sort order. Nulls sort low.

The order of the output rows can be changed from ascending to descending by specifying DESC to get a descending sort, as illustrated below.

```
SELECT     last_name
           ,class_code
FROM       student_table
ORDER BY class_code DESC;

Result: 10 rows returned

Last_name                 Class_code
--------------------      ----------
Phillips                  SR
Craig                     SR
McCann                    SO
McCormick                 SO
Rieter                    JR
Bond                      JR
Garrett                   FR
Kojack                    FR
Lamp                      FR
Johnson                   ?
```

Figure 2.5

Note: Nulls sort low.

When writing queries, it can become tedious having to write the same column name repeatedly. As a convenience, the SQL language allows you to use numeric designators to specify the output columns to be used for sorting.

The following example illustrates this. It uses the class_code column position instead of the column name.

```
SELECT      last_name
            ,class_code
FROM        student_table
ORDER BY 2 DESC;

Result: 10 rows returned

Last_name               Class_code
--------------------    ----------
Phillips                SR
Craig                   SR
McCann                  SO
McCormick               SO
Rieter                  JR
Bond                    JR
Garrett                 FR
Kojack                  FR
Lamp                    FR
Johnson                 ?
```

Figure 2.6

Note: Using numeric column designators should be discouraged. If the order of columns following SELECT changes, the system will still sort on whatever output column is in that position. Explicit column names will always be used regardless of their output position.

Multiple ORDER BY Columns

You are probably asking yourself these questions, "Can I mix ASCending and DESCending? Is the first column the major sort key?" The answer to both of these questions is "YES". The first column specified is the major sort column. The second and subsequent columns are minor sort columns. Separate the column names with commas.

The example below uses the column class_code as the major descending sort key, and the last_name column as an ascending sort key.

```
SELECT     last_name
           ,class_code
FROM       student_table
ORDER BY class_code DESC, last_name;

Result: 10 rows returned

Last_name                     Class_code
--------------------          ----------
Craig                         SR
Phillips                      SR
McCann                        SO
McCormick                     SO
Bond                          JR
Rieter                        JR
Garrett                       FR
Kojack                        FR
Lamp                          FR
Johnson                       ?
```

Figure 2.7

DISTINCT Option

Suppose you are interested in determining the unique values that exist in a column. You could list all of the rows and do a visual scan. If the table contains thousands of rows, having the system do the scan and report just the unique values, is a better solution.

The DISTINCT option specifies only one row is to be returned from any set of duplicates that might result from the query.

Two rows are considered duplicates only if each value in one is equal to each corresponding value in the other.

DISTINCT will return only one row for each specified value. The following example returns each distinct class code.

```
SELECT    DISTINCT class_code
FROM      student_table
ORDER BY class_code;

Result: 5 rows returned

Class_code
----------
?
FR
JR
SO
SR
```

Figure 2.8

When additional columns are added to the SELECT, a row will be returned for every value combination of the listed columns. As illustrated below, if multiple rows have the same class_code + grade_pt values, only one of the rows will be returned.

```
SELECT    DISTINCT class_code, grade_pt
FROM      student_table
ORDER BY class_code, grade_pt;

Result: 10 rows returned

Class_code  Grade_Pt
----------  --------
?                  ?
FR               .00
FR              2.88
FR              4.00
JR              1.90
JR              3.95
SO              2.00
SO              3.80
SR              3.00
SR              3.35
```

Figure 2.9

WHERE

Other than the DISTINCT option, all of the queries we've seen returned an output row for every table row. For small tables this is probably fine. However, for large tables you will probably want to limit the output to only those rows meeting certain criteria.

The WHERE clause enables you to retrieve only the rows you need, by specifying a search condition. The following illustrates the general layout of a query with a WHERE clause.

```
SELECT  <column-names>
FROM    <table-name>
WHERE <column-name> <comparison> <data-value> ;
```

Figure 2.10

The chart below lists the comparison operations that are available.

Comparison Operators:

OPERATOR	MEANING
=	Equal
< >	Not Equal
>	Greater Than
<	Less Than
>=	Greater Than or Equal To
<=	Less Than or Equal To
BETWEEN . . . AND	Inclusive range
[NOT] IN	Test against predefined set
IS [NOT] NULL	Test for nulls
EXISTS	Test for existence
LIKE	Test for partial string

Figure 2.11

The following example limits the output to only those students who have a grade_pt *Greater Than or Equal to* 3.0.

```
SELECT    student_id
        , last_name
        , grade_pt
FROM      student_table
WHERE     grade_pt >= 3.0 ;

Result: 5 rows returned

Student_ID  Last_name               Grade_Pt
----------- ----------------------  --------
    324652  Craig                       3.35
    231222  McCormick                   3.80
    234121  Garrett                     4.00
    322133  Bond                        3.95
    123250  Phillips                    3.00
```

Figure 2.12

Compound Comparisons

Suppose you want to retrieve only those rows meeting multiple conditions. You just can't put them into a comma-separated list like you can the column names in an Order By clause.

Complex comparisons are created by combining different comparisons using Logical operators to form compound comparisons.

Figure 2.13 lists the Logical Operators.

LOGICAL OPERATOR	MEANING
AND	All specified conditions must be met.
OR	Rows meeting either condition are selected.
NOT	Negates the specified condition or specified operator.

Figure 2.13

The following example shows the generic syntax of a query with a compound condition in the WHERE clause.

```
SELECT  <column-name>
FROM    <table-name>
WHERE  <column-name> <comparison> <data-value> { AND | OR }
        <column-name> <comparison> <data-value>;
```

Figure 2.14

Look at the following query, and see if you can determine how many rows will be returned.

```
SELECT    last_name
          , first_name
          , grade_pt
FROM      student_table
WHERE    grade_pt = 3.0 AND grade_pt = 4.0;
```

Figure 2.15

Remember, the AND operator says **both** conditions must be met. The OR condition says **either** condition must be met. Since a column in a row can only contain one value, the correct answer to the question is 'None'.

The following query changes the AND to OR and produces the output as shown.

```
SELECT    last_name
        , first_name
        , grade_pt
FROM      student_table
WHERE     grade_pt = 3.0 OR grade_pt = 4.0;

Result: 2 rows returned

Last_name                 First_name      Grade_Pt
-------------------       ------------    --------
Garrett                   Wendy               4.00
Phillips                  Beth                3.00
```

Figure 2.16

Using AND and OR

As the WHERE clause becomes more complex, the use of parentheses in coding compound conditional statements is vital to getting the correct results. Examine the following query and its output.

```
SELECT  last_name
        ,class_code
        ,grade_pt
FROM    student_table
WHERE  grade_pt = 3.0
    OR grade_pt = 4.0
   AND  class_code = 'FR' ;

Result: 2 rows returned

Last_name                 Class_code  Grade_Pt
--------------------      ----------  --------
Garrett                   FR              4.00
Phillips                  SR              3.00
```

Figure 2.17

Can you determine why Phillips was selected? He's not a FR(eshman).

The answer lies in knowing where the SQL Parser logically puts parentheses if you don't, as illustrated in Figure 2.18.

```
SELECT  last_name
        ,class_code
        ,grade_pt
FROM    student_table
WHERE  (grade_pt = 3.0)
       OR
       (grade_pt = 4.0 AND  class_code = 'FR') ;
```

Figure 2.18

As you can see, ORed conditions are treated separately from ANDed conditions. ANDed conditions are grouped together. So, to combine multiple OR conditions against a column and then have them ANDed to another test, use parentheses.

The example below illustrates this.

```
SELECT   last_name
         ,class_code
         ,grade_pt
FROM     student_table
WHERE    ( grade_pt = 3.0  OR  grade_pt = 4.0 )
         AND  class_code = 'FR' ;

Result: 1 row returned

Last_name                Class_code   Grade_Pt
--------------------     ----------   --------
Garrett                  FR               4.00
```

Figure 2.19

Using the NOT Operator

Sometimes it's difficult to figure out the inverse of a complex compound conditional phrase. The solution to this is to have the system figure it out for you. Simply put the entire conditional phrase inside a set of parentheses, and preface it with the NOT logical operator.

The following example utilizes both the NOT and the AND comparison in order to identify all seniors, along with lower classmates with grade points less than 3.0.

```
SELECT      last_name
            ,first_name
            ,class_code
            ,grade_pt
FROM        student_table
WHERE  NOT ( grade_pt >= 3.0
            AND class_code <> 'SR' ) ;

Result: 6 rows returned

Last_name                First_name     Class_code   Grade_Pt
--------------------     ------------   ----------   --------
Lamp                     Mike           FR                .00
McCann                   Andy           SO               2.00
Rieter                   Richard        JR               1.90
Kojack                   Henry          FR               2.88
Craig                    Danny          SR               3.35
Phillips                 Beth           SR               3.00
```

Figure 2.20

The NOT operator reverses condition testing, including changing the AND to OR.

The WHERE clause, above,
         WHERE NOT (grade_pt >= 3.0 AND class_code <> 'SR')
is equivalent to
         WHERE (grade_pt < 3.0 OR class_code = 'SR')

Comparisons Against Nulls

NULL represents the absence of a data value.
NULL indicates a column has no data.
NULL represents an unknown or non-existent value.
NULL is an SQL keyword.
NULL is neither a data type nor a characteristic of data.
NULL columns may be COMPRESSed to occupy zero space in a row.

The following chart shows the result of actions on nulls.

Col1	Operator	Col2	Result
10	+	NULL	NULL
10	-	NULL	NULL
10	*	NULL	NULL
10	/	NULL	NULL
10	>	NULL	Unknown/False
10	<	NULL	Unknown/False
10	>=	NULL	Unknown/False
10	<=	NULL	Unknown/False
10	=	NULL	Unknown/False
10	<>	NULL	Unknown/False
NULL	>	NULL	Unknown/False
NULL	<	NULL	Unknown/False
NULL	>=	NULL	Unknown/False
NULL	<=	NULL	Unknown/False
NULL	=	NULL	Unknown/False
NULL	<>	NULL	Unknown/False

Figure 2.21

Based upon the chart above, the next query will return zero rows.

```
SELECT  student_id
      , last_name
      , grade_pt
      , class_code
FROM student_table
WHERE  grade_pt = NULL  AND class_code = NULL ;
```

Figure 2.22

Simply change the equal sign to the reserved word IS.

```
SELECT  student_id
      , last_name
      , grade_pt
      , class_code
FROM student_table
WHERE  grade_pt IS NULL  AND class_code IS NULL ;

Result: 1 row returned

Student_ID  Last_name                Grade_Pt  Class_code
-----------  -------------------      --------  ----------
    260000   Johnson                       ?   ?
```

Figure 2.23

Note: Numeric data is right-aligned and character data is left-aligned. This includes the default symbol (?) for a null.

Using IN and NOT IN

Suppose you want to test a column for multiple values. You could write multiple ORed comparisons, such as

WHERE <col> <condition> <val1> OR <col> <condition> <val2> OR ...

The IN comparison operator is an easier alternative to using OR comparisons (requires less typing than the OR) and allows values to be listed within parenthesis. This is illustrated in the following query.

```
SELECT      last_name
          , class_code
          , grade_pt
FROM        student_table
WHERE       grade_pt IN ( 2.0, 3.0, 4.0 );

Result: 3 rows returned

Last_name              Class_code   Grade_Pt
-------------------    ----------   --------
Garrett                FR               4.00
McCann                 SO               2.00
Phillips               SR               3.00
```

Figure 2.24

To reverse the logic, simply use NOT IN as shown below.

```
SELECT       last_name
           , class_code
           , grade_pt
FROM       student_table
WHERE      grade_pt NOT IN ( 2.0, 3.0, 4.0 ) ;

Result: 6 rows returned

Last_name               Class_code   Grade_Pt
--------------------    ----------   --------
Lamp                    FR                .00
McCormick               SO               3.80
Rieter                  JR               1.90
Bond                    JR               3.95
Kojack                  FR               2.88
Craig                   SR               3.35
```

Figure 2.25

Using BETWEEN

There is another conditional operator, called BETWEEN, that can be used to test a column for values within a given range.

BETWEEN is simpler than either a compound OR comparison, or an IN comparison (a lengthy value list of sequential numbers would be required). A query using the BETWEEN comparison operator is shown below in Figure 2.26.

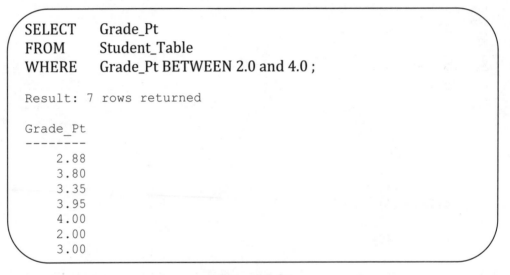

```
SELECT     Grade_Pt
FROM       Student_Table
WHERE      Grade_Pt BETWEEN 2.0 and 4.0 ;

Result: 7 rows returned

Grade_Pt
--------
    2.88
    3.80
    3.35
    3.95
    4.00
    2.00
    3.00
```

Figure 2.26

An important thing to remember is that BETWEEN is inclusive. Notice, in the above example, that 2.0 and 4.0 are included in the answer set.

Using the LIKE operator

Another frequently used comparison operator is the LIKE operator. The LIKE operator can only be used to search for a string of consecutive characters within character data. It cannot be used on numeric data.

The following shows the general syntax and meaning of the LIKE components.

Syntax: *expression* [NOT] LIKE [ALL | ANY | SOME] *pattern_expression* [ESCAPE *escape_character*]

Syntax Element . . .	Specifies . . .
expression	a character string or character string expression argument to be searched for the substring *pattern_expression.*
pattern_expression	a character expression for which *expression* is to be searched.
ANY SOME	Compares a value to each value in a list and returned by a query. SOME is a synonym for ANY.
ALL	Compares a single value against a set of data from a query.
ESCAPE *escape_character*	a keyword/variable combination specifying a single escape character.

Figure 2.27

In creating a search pattern, you can use wildcard characters to represent one or more characters that can be ignored by the comparison logic.

The following chart describes the wildcard characters and their meaning.

Character	Description
% (Percent sign)	Represents any string of zero or more arbitrary characters. Any string of characters is acceptable as a replacement for the percent.
_ (Underscore)	Represents exactly one arbitrary character. Any single character is acceptable in the position in which the underscore character appears, but a character must exist in that position.

Figure 2.28

The following example returns all employee rows where the last name of the employee begins with 'St'.

```
SELECT last_name
FROM   employee_table
WHERE last_name  LIKE 'St%' ;

Result: 2 rows returned

Last_name
-------------------
Student
Strickland
```

Figure 2.29

In doing comparisons against character data, it is vital to know whether you are running in Teradata (BT/ET) transaction mode, or in ANSI transaction mode. The issue is case sensitivity. Teradata is NOT CASESPECIFIC, whereas ANSI is CASESPECIFIC.

The results from the following query illustrate this issue.

```
SELECT last_name
FROM   employee_table
WHERE last_name  LIKE 'st%' ;

In BTET transaction mode:

Result: 2 rows returned

Last_name
--------------------
Student
Strickland

In ANSI transaction mode:

*** Query completed. No rows found.
*** Total elapsed time was 1 second.
```

Figure 2.30

Practice Questions

1. NULL values always sort high?
   a. TRUE
   b. FALSE

2. Which of the following ORDER BY clauses is invalid?
   a. 3 DESC, 2 ASC, 5
   b. 6, 2, 4 ASC, 1
   c. 2, 6, DESC 3, 7
   d. 2, 3, 4, 2

3. Where will the Parser logically put parenthesis in the following?
   a. WHERE A = 1 OR B = 2 AND C = 3 OR D = 4
   b. WHERE (A = 1 OR B = 2) AND (C = 3 OR D = 4)
   c. WHERE A = 1) OR (B = 2) AND (C = 3) OR (D = 4)
   d. WHERE (A = 1) OR (B = 2 AND C = 3) OR (D = 4)

4. WHERE A IN (1, 8) defines an inclusive range.
   a. TRUE
   b. FALSE

5. Which statement is true?
   a. The LIKE operator requires both operands to be numeric.
   b. The LIKE operator requires both operands to be character.
   c. The LIKE operator requires at least one operand to be numeric.

6. Which statement is true?
   a. Teradata is not CASESPECIFIC, and ANSI is not CASESPECIFIC.
   b. Teradata is not CASESPECIFIC, and ANSI is CASESPECIFIC.
   c. Teradata is CASESPECIFIC, and ANSI is CASESPECIFIC.
   d. Teradata is CASESPECIFIC, and ANSI is not CASESPECIFIC.

Chapter Notes

Utilize this space for notes, key points to remember, diagrams, areas of further study, etc.

_____

_____

_____

_____

_____

_____

_____

_____

_____

_____

_____

_____

_____

_____

Chapter 3: HELP, SHOW, EXPLAIN Commands

Certification Objectives

✓ Describe usage of HELP, SHOW, and EXPLAIN commands and their expected outputs.

Before You Begin

You should be familiar with the following terms and concepts.

Terms	Key Concepts
HELP	How to use the HELP commands
SHOW	Understand the types of SHOW commands
EXPLAIN	What are the key concepts of an Explain

HELP Commands

What columns does this table contain? What objects are stored in this database? Is my session in Teradata transaction mode or ANSI transaction mode? Whenever you need information like this, all you need to do is to ask for HELP.

The HELP commands display information about:

- Database objects
- Session Characteristics
- SQL syntax

The following charts in Figure 3.1, describe the various HELP commands.

Databases and Users:

HELP DATABASE	Returns information about objects stored in the database.
HELP USER	Returns information about objects stored in the user.

Tables, Views, and Macros:

HELP TABLE	Returns detailed information about the columns in the table.
HELP VIEW	Returns the list of columns in the view.
HELP MACRO	Returns information about the parameters of the macro.
HELP COLUMN	Returns detailed information about the column or columns requested.
HELP INDEX	Returns detailed information about all indexes on a table.
HELP STATISTICS	Returns the date and time statistics were last collected or refreshed, how many distinct values were present, and which column(s) statistics were collected on.
HELP CONSTRAINT	Returns detailed information about the constraint.
HELP SESSION ;	Returns detailed information about the user's session.
HELP 'SQL';	SQL command syntax help list.
HELP 'SPL';	Stored Procedure command syntax help list.

Figure 3.1

The following charts provide you with some syntax examples to help you get started.

Databases and Users

HELP DATABASE	CSQL_CLASS;
HELP USER	CSQL01;

Figure 3.2

Tables, Views, and Macros

HELP TABLE	employee_table ;
HELP VIEW	employee_v ;
HELP MACRO	new_sales ;
HELP COLUMN	* FROM employee_table ; employee_table.* ; employee_table.last_name ; CSQL_VIEWS.employee_v.* ; CSQL_VIEWS.employee_v.last_name ;
HELP INDEX	employee_table ;
HELP STATISTICS	employee_table ;
HELP CONSTRAINT	employee_table.over_21 ;
HELP SESSION ;	

Figure 3.3

HELP DATABASE

The following figure shows a HELP DATABASE command and the information returned by the system.

```
HELP DATABASE CSQL_CLASS;

Table/View/Macro name           Kind Comment
------------------------------- ---- ------------------
b_words                           T    ?
Course_table                      T    ?
Customer_table                    T    ?
date_time                         T    ?
Department_table                  T    ?
Employee_table                    T    ?
Emp_Job_table                     T    ?
Job_table                         T    ?
Names_table                       T    ?
Order_table                       T    ?
Sales_table                       T    ?
Stats_Table                       T    ?
Student_Course_table              T    ?
Student_table                     T    ?
```

Figure 3.4

HELP TABLE

The HELP command in Figure 3.4 returns information about the columns in the employee_table. The chart in Figure 3.5 describes the meaning of the Type code shown as the second column of output.

```
HELP TABLE employee_table ;

Column Name                          Type Comment
------------------------------------ ---- -----------
Employee_No                          I    Primary Key
Dept_No                              I2   Foreign Key
Mgr_Employee_No                      I    Foreign Key
Last_name                            CF
First_name                           CV
Salary                               D    ?
```

Figure 3.5

Data types on the HELP TABLE are:

Type	Description
CF	CHARACTER FIXED
CV	CHARACTER VARIABLE
D	DECIMAL
DA	DATE
I	INTEGER
I1	BYTEINT
I2	SMALLINT

Figure 3.6

HELP 'SQL'

The system has a built-in syntax guide that is available through the following HELP command. Notice that SQL must be inside of single quotes. The output shown is just a partial listing.

```
HELP 'SQL' ;

On-Line Help
----------------------------------------------------------------------

DBS SQL COMMANDS:

ABORT                   ALTER FUNCTION              ALTER METHOD
ALTER PROCEDURE         ALTER REPLICATION GROUP     ALTER TABLE
ALTER TRIGGER           ALTER TYPE                  BEGIN LOGGING
BEGIN QUERY LOGGING     BEGIN TRANSACTION           CALL
CHECKPOINT              COLLECT DEMOGRAPHICS        COLLECT STATISTICS
COMMENT                 COMMIT                      CREATE AUTHORIZATION
CREATE CAST             CREATE DATABASE             CREATE FUNCTION

 .  .  .

DBS SQL FUNCTIONS:

ABS                     ADD_MONTHS                  ACOS
ACOSH                   ASIN                        ASINH
ATAN                    ATANH                       ATAN2
AVERAGE                 BYTES                       CAST
CASE_N                  CHAR_LENGTH                 CHAR2HEXINT
CHARACTERS              COS                         COSH
COUNT                   CORR                        COVAR_POP

 .  .  .
```

Figure 3.7

SHOW Commands

Though the HELP command returns useful information, it sometimes lacks the detail needed. To get the most information about an object, the SHOW command displays the actual CREATE syntax.

The following chart lists a few of the SHOW commands. To get a complete list, do HELP 'SQL SHOW';

Command	Returns
SHOW TABLE tablename ;	CREATE TABLE statement
SHOW VIEW viewname ;	CREATE VIEW statement
SHOW MACRO macroname ;	CREATE MACRO statement
. . .	

Figure 3.8

SHOW TABLE

The SHOW TABLE commands return the fully expanded CREATE TABLE syntax. Compare the detail provided by the following SHOW command to the HELP command in Figure 3.4.

```
SHOW TABLE employee_table ;

CREATE SET TABLE CSQL_CLASS.employee_table ,NO FALLBACK ,
     NO BEFORE JOURNAL,
     NO AFTER JOURNAL,
     CHECKSUM = DEFAULT
     (
      Employee_No INTEGER,
      Dept_No SMALLINT,
      Mgr_Employee_No INTEGER,
      Last_name CHAR(20) CHARACTER SET LATIN
              NOT CASESPECIFIC,
      First_name VARCHAR(12) CHARACTER SET LATIN
              NOT CASESPECIFIC,
      Salary DECIMAL(8,2))
UNIQUE PRIMARY INDEX ( Employee_No )
INDEX ( Last_name )
INDEX ( Dept_No );
```

Figure 3.9

SHOW VIEW

Unlike the SHOW TABLE, the SHOW VIEW command returns just the syntax that was entered to create the view, exactly the way it was entered. This is illustrated by the following example.

```
SHOW VIEW CSQL_VIEWS.customer_v ;

CV  CSQL_VIEWS.Customer_v  (Cust_no, Cust_name, Phone)  AS
sel  customer_number, Customer_name, Phone_number
from CSQL_CLASS.customer_table;
```

Figure 3.10

SHOW MACRO

The following example shows the output from a SHOW MACRO command.

```
SHOW MACRO enrollments;

Create macro enrollments as
(select last_name
     ,first_name
     ,sc.course_id
     ,course_name
From      student_table as s
Inner join
     Student_course_table as sc
On    s.student_id = sc.student_id
Inner join
     Course_table c
On    sc.course_id = c.course_id
Order by sc.course_id, last_name;
);
```

Figure 3.11

EXPLAIN

When the word EXPLAIN appears in front of any SQL statement, the statement is fully parsed, but instead of the execution plan being sent to the AMPs, it is sent to the Explain facility which translates the processing steps into English and returns the translation to the user.

EXPLAIN is a powerful tool to help understand what the system will do if the SQL is actually executed.

The following is an example of an EXPLAIN of a simple SELECT.

EXPLAIN SELECT * FROM employee_table ;

```
*** Help information returned. 12 rows.
 *** Total elapsed time was 1 second.

Explanation
-------------------------------------------------------------------
  1)  First, we lock a distinct CSQL_CLASS."pseudo table" for read
      on a RowHash to prevent global deadlock for
      CSQL_CLASS.employee_table.
  2) Next, we lock CSQL_CLASS.employee_table for read.
  3) We do an all-AMPs RETRIEVE step from
     CSQL_CLASS.employee_table by way of an all-rows scan with no
     residual conditions into Spool 1 (group_amps), which is built
     locally on the AMPs.  The size of Spool 1 is estimated with
     low confidence to be 12 rows (1,092 bytes).  The estimated
     time for this step is 0.03 seconds.
  4) Finally, we send out an END TRANSACTION step to all AMPs
     involved in processing the request.
  >   The contents of Spool 1 are sent back to the user as the
      result of statement 1.  The total estimated time is 0.03
      seconds.
```

Figure 3.12

EXPLAIN Terminology

Most EXPLAIN text is easy to understand. The following additional definitions may be helpful:

TERM	MEANING
... (Last Use) ...	A spool file is no longer needed and will be released when this step completes.
... with no residual conditions ...	All applicable conditions have been applied to the rows.
... END TRANSACTION ...	Transaction locks are released, and changes are committed.
... eliminating duplicate rows ...	(Duplicate rows only exist in spool files, not set tables.) Doing a DISTINCT operation.
... by way of the sort key in spool field1 ...	Field1 is created to allow a tag sort.
... we do an ABORT test ...	Caused by an ABORT or ROLLBACK statement.
... by way of a traversal of index #n extracting row ids only ...	A spool file is built containing the Row IDs found in a secondary index (index #n).
... we do a SMS (set manipulation step) ...	Combining rows using a UNION, EXCEPT, or INTERSECT operator.
... we do a BMSMS (bit map set manipulation step)	Doing a NUSI Bit Map operation.
... which is redistributed by hash code to all AMPs. ... which is duplicated on all AMPs.	Relocating data in preparation for a join.
... (one_AMP) or (group_AMPs)	indicates one AMP or a subset of AMPs will be used instead of all AMPs.
... ("NOT	feature in which the optimizer

(table_name.column_name IS NULL)")	realizes that the column being joined to is NOT NULL or has referential integrity.
... Joined using a row id join ...	indicates a join back condition with a join index.

Figure 3.13

The various "confidence" phrases and their meaning are provided in the following chart.

PHRASE	MEANING
. . . with high confidence . . .	– Restricting conditions exist on index(es) or column(s) that have collected statistics.
. . . with low confidence . . .	– Restricting conditions exist on index(es) having no statistics, but estimates can be based upon a sampling of the index(es). – Restricting conditions exist on index(es) or column(s) that have collected statistics but are "ANDed" together with conditions on non-indexed columns. – Restricting conditions exist on index(es) or column(s) that have collected statistics but are "ORed" together with other conditions.
. . . with no confidence . . .	– Conditions outside the above.

Figure 3.14

Practice Questions

1. Which of the following will return online syntax for the ABORT command?
    a. HELP ABORT;
    b. HELP 'ABORT';
    c. HELP 'SQL ABORT';

2. You cannot EXPLAIN "EXPLAIN".
    a. TRUE
    b. FALSE

3. SHOW DATABASE is a valid SQL command.
    a. TRUE
    b. FALSE

4. The timings provided by EXPLAIN represent:
    a. Measured clock time.
    b. Cost estimates for comparison purposes.

5. The term "no residual conditions" means:
    a. All applicable conditions have been applied to the rows.
    b. There were no conditions specified.

6. A "high confidence" phrase requires statistics on the restricting columns or indexes.
    a. TRUE
    b. FALSE

Chapter Notes

Utilize this space for notes, key points to remember, diagrams, areas of further study, etc.

_____

_____

_____

_____

_____

_____

_____

_____

_____

_____

_____

_____

_____

_____

Chapter 4: Data Conversions

Certification Objectives

- ✓ Given a scenario, identify the ramifications of converting from one data type to another.
- ✓ Explain the data type conversions as a result of computations.
- ✓ Given a scenario using CAST, identify the proper result.
- ✓ Given a value, identify the answer that is returned for mathematical vs. accounting ROUNDING.
- ✓ Identify formatting options for internationalization of various data types.

Before You Begin

You should be familiar with the following terms and concepts.

Terms	Key Concepts
Data Types	What are the data types supported and how to do conversions
Rounding	How is this handled with decimal data
Formatting	Options available including internationalizations

Data Types

All data in a database will have characteristics associated with it called attributes. Attributes would include a data type and length. A data type specifies the type and format of the data. The data value must conform to the rules and characteristics of the data type. A column in a relational database may only store one type of data and data types may not be mixed. Teradata supports most standard ANSI data types.

Teradata allows you to use either the specific data type name, or the data type alias when defining a column's data type, but will actually use the full data type name in the table definition. Teradata will convert data types when necessary.

The following charts, of Figure 4.1, show the characteristics of the supported data types.

Byte Data	Description
BLOB	Binary Large Object Max: 2,097,088,000 bytes which is the default
BYTE (size)	Fixed length Binary string. Default: (1) Max: 64,000 bytes
VARBYTE (size)	Variable length Binary string. Default: (1) Max: 64,000 bytes

Numeric Data	Description
BIGINT	8 bytes with the least significant byte first
BYTEINT	Whole number Range: -128 to 127 1 byte
SMALLINT	Whole number Range: -32,768 to 32,767 2 bytes
INTEGER	Whole number. Range: -2,147,483,648 to 2,147,483,647 4 bytes
DECIMAL [(n[,m])]	Decimal number of n digits, with m digits to the right of the decimal point. Default: DECIMAL(5,0)

	Number of digits (n)	Number of bytes
	1 to 2	1
	3 to 4	2
	5 to 9	4
	10 to 18	8
	19 to 38	16
NUMERIC [(n [, m])]	Synonym for DECIMAL	
FLOAT (n)	Floating Point number. IEEE format. Range: $2.226*10^{-308}$ to $1.797*10^{308}$ 8 bytes	
DOUBLE PRECISION	Synonym for FLOAT	
REAL	Synonym for FLOAT	

Date/Time	Description
DATE	Special type of integer. (((Calendar year) – 1900) * 10000) + MM * 100 + DD. Use ANSI Date form for compatibility. 4 bytes
TIME (n)	Stored as HHMMSS.nnnnnn 6 bytes
TIMESTAMP (n)	Stored as YYMMDDHHMMSS.nnnnnn 10 bytes
TIME (n) WITH TIME ZONE	Stored as HHMMSS.nnnnnn+HHMM 8 bytes
TIMESTAMP (n) WITH TIME ZONE	Stored as YYMMDDHHMMSS.nnnnnn+HHMM 12 bytes

Interval data types	Description
INTERVAL YEAR [(n)]	Number of years (n) = 1 to 4 digits for years Default = 2 2 bytes
INTERVAL MONTH [(n)]	Number of months (n) = 1 to 4 digits for months Default = 2 2 bytes
INTERVAL DAY [(n)]	Number of days (n) = 1 to 4 digits for days Default = 2 2 bytes
INTERVAL YEAR [(n)] TO MONTH	Number of years and months (n) = 1 to 4 digits for years Default = 2 4 bytes
INTERVAL HOUR [(n)]	Number of hours (n) = 1 to 4 digits for years Default = 2 2 bytes
INTERVAL MINUTE [(n)]	Number of minutes (n) = 1 to 4 digits for days Default = 2 2 bytes
INTERVAL SECOND [(n)]	Number of seconds (n) = 1 to 4 digits for days Default = 2 (m) = 0 to 6 digits for fractional seconds Default = 6 6 bytes
INTERVAL DAY [(n)] TO HOUR	Number of days and hours (n) = 1 to 4 digits for days Default = 2 4 bytes

INTERVAL DAY [(n)] TO MINUTE	Number of days, hours and minutes (n) = 1 to 4 digits for days Default = 2 HOUR is always 2 digits and MINUTE is always 2 digits 8 bytes
INTERVAL DAY [(n)] TO SECOND [(m)]	Number of days, hours, minutes, and seconds (n) = 1 to 4 digits for days Default = 2 (m) = 0 to 6 digits for fractional seconds Default = 6 10 bytes
INTERVAL HOUR TO MINUTE	Number of hours and minutes (n) = 1 to 4 digits for hours Default = 2 4 bytes
INTERVAL HOUR [(n)] TO SECOND [(m)]	Number of hours, minutes and seconds (n) = 1 to 4 digits for hours Default = 2 (m) = 0 to 6 digits for fractional seconds Default = 6 8 bytes
INTERVAL MINUTE [(n)] TO SECOND [(m)]	Number of minutes and seconds (n) = 1 to 4 digits for minutes Default = 2 (m) = 0 to 6 digits for fractional seconds Default = 6 6 bytes

Character / Graphic Data Types	Description
CHAR (size)	Fixed length character data. Max: 64,000
CLOB	Character Large Object Max: 2,097,088,000 which is the default
VARCHAR (size) or CHARACTER VARYING (size)	Variable length character data Max: 64,000
LONG VARCHAR	Equivalent to VARCHAR(64000)
GRAPHIC (size)	Fixed length graphic data. 2 bytes per character Max: 32,000 double-byte characters
LONG VARGRAPHIC	Fixed length graphic data. 32,000 double-byte characters
VARGRAPHIC (size)	Variable length graphic data. 2 bytes per character Max: 32,000 double-byte characters

Figure 4.1

Note:

1. DATE is supported both in its Teradata form and in the preferred ANSI DateTime form. For new development, define DATE using ANSI DATE type.
2. The GRAPHIC types are equivalent to the type CHARACTER SET GRAPHIC, which is the form to use for all new development.
3. The CREATE TYPE statement determines the name of a UDT.

Data Conversions

Normally, operands must be of the same data type to do a comparison. One of the powerful abilities of Teradata SQL is the ability to compare operands of different data types. If two operands are not of the same data type, Teradata will automatically convert one, or both, to a common data type and then do the comparison.

As an example, comparisons between character and numeric data types require that the character field be convertible to a numeric value.
Implicit conversions (implied CAST) are a Teradata extension to the ANSI SQL-2003 standard.

If operand data types differ, then the Teradata Database performs an implied CAST according to the following table in Figure 4.2.

IF one expression operand is . . .	AND the other expression operand is . . .	THEN Teradata compares the data as . . .
Character	Character	Character
Character	Date	Date
Character	BYTEINT SMALLINT INTEGER FLOAT	FLOAT
CHAR(k) VARCHAR(k) where k <= 16	BIGINT DECIMAL (m,n) where m <= 16	FLOAT
BYTEINT	SMALLINT	SMALLINT
BYTEINT SMALLINT	INTEGER	INTEGER
BYTEINT SMALLINT	BIGINT	BIGINT

INTEGER BIGINT		
BYTEINT	DECIMAL (m,n) where m <= 18 and m-n >= 3	DECIMAL (18,n)
SMALLINT	DECIMAL (m,n) where m <= 18 and m-n >= 5	DECIMAL (18,n)
INTEGER DATE	DECIMAL (m,n) where m <= 18 and m-n >= 10	DECIMAL (18,n)
BYTEINT	DECIMAL (m,n) where m > 18 or m-n < 3	DECIMAL(38, n)
SMALLINT	DECIMAL (m,n) where m > 18 or m-n < 5	DECIMAL(38, n)
INTEGER DATE	DECIMAL (m,n) where m > 18 or m-n < 10	DECIMAL(38, n)
BIGINT	DECIMAL(m,n)	DECIMAL(38, n)
DECIMAL (m,n)	DECIMAL(k,j) where max($m-n,k-j$) + max(j,n) <= 18	DECIMAL(18,max(j,n))
DECIMAL (m,n)	DECIMAL(k,j) where max($m-n,k-j$) + max(j,n) > 18	DECIMAL(38,max(j,n))
DATE	BYTEINT SMALLINT	INTEGER

	INTEGER	
DATE	BIGINT	BIGINT
DATE	FLOAT	FLOAT
FLOAT	BYTEINT SMALLINT INTEGER BIGINT DECIMAL(m,n)	FLOAT

Figure 4.2

CAST

When writing a query, it is sometimes necessary to redefine a data type. For example, a column with a character data type containing date information might need to be converted into a date data type in order to perform date calculations.

In the following example, notice that character data is left justified and numeric data is right justified.

```
SELECT CAST('ABCDE' AS CHAR(2) )  AS C1
        ,CAST(129 AS CHAR(6))  AS C2
        ,CAST(127 AS BYTEINT) AS B1
        ,CAST(128 AS SMALLINT)  AS S1
        ,CAST(129 AS INTEGER )  AS I1;

Result: 1 row returned

C1   C2         B1      S1              I1
--   ------     ----    ------    -----------
AB   129        127     128             129
```

Figure 4.3

Teradata 12 Certification Study Guide

Notice that Teradata mode allowed the string value in the first line to be truncated. In ANSI mode, truncation of string data is forbidden, so the first line of the query would cause the entire query to fail with the following error message.

```
*** Failure 3996 Right truncation of string data.
```

By eliminating any truncation of string data, the query will work.

```
SELECT CAST('ABCDE' AS CHAR(6) )  AS C1
       ,CAST(129 AS CHAR(6))  AS C2
       ,CAST(127 AS BYTEINT) AS B1
       ,CAST(128 AS SMALLINT)  AS S1
       ,CAST(129 AS INTEGER )  AS I1;

Result: 1 row returned

C1        C2        B1      S1                I1
------    ------    ----    ------    -----------
ABCDE     129       127     128               129
```

Figure 4.4

Rounding

The rounding of fractional decimal values plays an important role in many financial and scientific calculations. Understanding the rules governing rounding becomes important to achieving the correct results.

The following chart describes how rounding is accomplished by Teradata.

IF the value of the digit to the right of the rounding digit is . . .	THEN the value of the rounding digit . . .
<5	does not change
>5	increases by one

IF the value of the digit to the right of the rounding digit is exactly 5 and . . .	THEN . . .		
there are no trailing non-zero digits	IF the value of the rounding digit is . . .	THEN the value of the rounding digit . . .	
	Odd	Increases by one	
	Even	Does not change	
there are trailing non-zero digits	rounding behaves as if the value of the digit to the right of the rounding digit is greater than five		

Figure 4.5

The following query demonstrates these rules.

```
SELECT CAST(.014 AS DECIMAL(3,2))
       ,CAST(.015 AS DECIMAL(3,2))
       ,CAST(.025 AS DECIMAL(3,2))
       ,CAST(.0251 AS DECIMAL(3,2))
       ,CAST(.026 AS DECIMAL(3,2)) ;

Result: 1 row returned

.014    .015    .025    .0251    .026
-----   -----   -----   -----    -----
  .01     .02     .02     .03      .03
```

Figure 4.6

FORMAT

One of the relational database design guidelines is to store numbers in numeric data types. Following this guideline makes manipulating and searching the data easier. When it comes time to use these numeric columns in a report, being able to format the data makes it easier for end users to read the information. As an example, 832296468440.78 versus $832,296,468,440.78.

Teradata has an extension called FORMAT. It can be used with the Basic Teradata Query (BTEQ) tool to override the default format of data, both input and output. FORMAT cannot be used to specify any data conversions. SQL Assistant does not recognize the FORMAT clause.

The syntax is (FORMAT 'edit mask')

The following chart shows some of the various symbols that may be used to create an edit mask.

Symbol	Meaning
$	Fixed or floating dollar sign
9	Decimal digit (no zero suppression)
Z	Zero-suppressed decimal digit
,	Comma – insert where specified
.	Decimal point position
-	Dash character – insert where specified
/	Slash character – insert where specified
%	Percent character – insert where specified
X	Character data – each X represents one character
G	Graphic data – each G represents on logical (double-byte) character
B	Blank data – insert a space and this point

Figure 4.7

In the following example, the multiple dollar signs ($) represent a floating dollar sign. The nines (9) represent an actual digit, even if it is a zero (0).

```
SELECT  salary(FORMAT '$$$,$$9.99')
FROM    employee_table
WHERE  employee_no = 1324657 ;


Result: 1 row returned

    Salary
----------
$42,788.88
```

Figure 4.8

Management has decided to give everyone in department number 400 a $1,000 raise, and wants to know what percentage pay increase that represents.

```
SELECT   last_name AS Employee
       , salary (FORMAT'$$$$$$$.99') AS "Current Salary"
       , (1000/salary) * 100
             (FORMAT 'ZZ9%')
             (TITLE 'Percent//Increase')
FROM     employee_table
WHERE  dept_no = 400
ORDER BY 2
;


Result: 3 rows returned          .
                                              Percent
Employee                 Current Salary    Increase
--------------------     --------------    --------
Clooney                      $35000.00         3%
Strickland                   $54590.00         2%
Ford                         $54590.00         2%
```

Figure 4.9

In the above query there are some things to notice:
- The Z characters represent zero suppression.
- There is a TITLE clause. The syntax is (TITLE '<value>')
- TITLEs cannot be referenced within a query.
- The double slant characters (//) can be used to stack the words in a TITLE up to three lines.

The following chart provides you with an opportunity to see if you understand the proper use of the FORMAT clause.

FORMAT	Data	Result?
FORMAT '999999'	08777	
FORMAT 'ZZZZZ9'	08777	
FORMAT '999-9999'	6494123	
FORMAT 'X(3)'	'Smith'	
FORMAT '$$9.99'	73.85	
FORMAT '999.99'	73.85	
FORMAT 'X(2)'	73.85	
FORMAT 'X(2)'	'73.85'	

Figure 4.10

Date Formats

There are two different ways to display dates. They are the ANSI recommended format of

FORMAT 'YYYY-MM-DD'

And the Teradata default format of

FORMAT 'YY/MM/DD'

Date formats that only display two digits of the year are not recommended. You should use the ANSI format for compatibility.

Some other ways of formatting dates:

Syntax	Result
FORMAT 'YYYY/MM/DD'	2010/07/26
FORMAT 'DDbMMMbYYYY'	26 Jul 2010
FORMAT 'mmmBdd,Byyyy'	Jul 26, 2010
FORMAT 'dd.mm.yyyy'	26.07.2010

Figure 4.11

As stated earlier, SQL Assistant does not recognize the FORMAT clause. Instead, the SQL Assistant provides the user with a choice of date display formats. Go to **Tools -> Options -> General tab**. There you can specify one of the following formats:

Display dates in this format	Setting
Local	Uses Windows format 07/25/2010
YYYY-MM-DD	This matches the ANSI format 2010-07-25
DD/MMM/YYYY	25/Jul/2010
DD/MM/YYYY	25/07/2010
MM/DD/YYYY	07/25/2010
YYYY/MM/DD	2010/07/25

Figure 4.12

Extracting Portions of Dates

The FORMAT clause can be used to extract portions of dates. However, since dates are stored as an Integer, you can also use normal integer arithmetic to do the same thing. In addition, there is also an EXTRACT function (shown below) that will be discussed in a later chapter.

The example below illustrates some of the EXTRACT methods.

```
SELECT order_date AS TDAT_Default
      , order_date (FORMAT 'yyyy-mm-dd')
             AS ANSI_Format
      , order_date (FORMAT 'MMM-DD')
             AS Format_Extract
      , order_date/100 MOD 100 AS Calc_Month
      , EXTRACT (MONTH FROM order_date) AS EXTRACT_Month
FROM order_table
ORDER BY 1;


Result: 6 rows returned

TDAT_Default  ANSI_Format   Format_Extract   Calc_Month   EXTRACT_Month
------------  -----------   --------------   ----------   -------------
          ?            ?                ?            ?               ?
   07/01/01   2007-01-01           Jan-01            1               1
   07/05/04   2007-05-04           May-04            5               5
   07/09/09   2007-09-09           Sep-09            9               9
   07/10/01   2007-10-01           Oct-01           10              10
   07/10/10   2007-10-10           Oct-10           10              10
```

Figure 4.13

Notice how confusing a date can appear with only two digits of the year displayed.

User Defined Functions (UDFs)

A User Defined Function (UDF) is a compiled function, which can perform calculations and complete SQL commands, and are invoked as expressions from within SQL statements. UDFs are stored on their parent database/user's permanent space.

Teradata UDFs can be scalar functions that return single values, aggregate functions that return summary tables and table functions that return tables. UDFs are written in either the C or C++ programming language and must be compiled.

UDFs are very useful for performing calculations and summarizations of data. The ability to program in C or C++ allows for extended programming capability, beyond that of SQL. Examples of UDFs might include a function that checks if a value is numeric or a function that converts Fahrenheit into Celsius.

User Defined Types (UDTs)

A User Defined Type (UDT) is a custom data type that is defined by a user, often based on application or business rules. UDTs are usually a combination of one or more data types to form a new data type. UDTs reside in the Teradata SYSUDTLIB database, which is stored in permanent space. Teradata allows for two types of UDTs -- distinct and structured.

A distinct UDT is essentially a synonym for a regular Teradata type, such as a VARCHAR or INTEGER. A distinct UDT is useful when defining the data type for a column that may appear throughout a database. For instance, assume that customer id (cust_id) is used throughout several tables in our database, and it should always be assigned as an INTEGER. Unfortunately, it is very possible that two different table designing users might set the data types differently. By creating a distinct UDT for customer id, the table designing users would choose that UDT as the data type, as opposed to determining their own data type. Using the UDT ensures consistency across the data model for our customer id column.

A structured UDT is a made up of more than one different data types or UDTs. Structured UDTs are useful for creating custom data types that are specific to your application. For example, a structured UDT might be a unique identifier made up of a date, an integer value, and a character value (2008-12-3105STE).

Formatting for UDT

If you specify a FORMAT phrase to define the format for UDT columns, the format must be valid for the external type of the UDT, as specified by the transform that defines how to pass the UDT between the application and the server.

Formatting for Internationalizations

There is a *Specification for Data Formatting* (SDF) file available to the System Administrator. In addition to defining the default display formats for numeric, date, time, and timestamp data types, the SDF file defines strings that the Teradata Database displays in place of certain formatting characters that appear in a FORMAT phrase. The SDF file controls how the following kinds of information are formatted in the output.

- Day names
- Month names
- AM and PM names
- Numeric and currency separators
- Numeric and currency digit grouping rules
- Currency symbols
- Default display formats for data types

The SDF file also controls the default display formats for the following data types:

- BYTEINT
- SMALLINT
- BIGINT
- INTEGER
- NUMERIC and DECIMAL

- REAL, DOUBLE PRECISION, and FLOAT
- DATE
- TIME and TIME WITH TIME ZONE
- TIMESTAMP and TIMESTAMP WITH TIME ZONE

Note: You cannot use the SDF file to control output formatting for the INTERVAL data type.

Practice Questions

1. With 00000.87 as input, which FORMAT mask will produce the following result:
   a. $0.87
   b. '$$$,$$$.99'
   c. '$$$,$$9.99'
   d. 'ZZZZZ9.99'
   e. 'ZZZZ$9.99'

2. Which result will CAST(.254 AS DECIMAL (2,2)) produce?
   a. 0.25
   b. 0.26

3. In ANSI transaction mode, CAST('Teradata' AS CHAR(4)) will produce:
   a. An error
   b. Tera

4. CAST(12345 AS CHAR(5)) – CAST(123 AS DEC(3,0)) will produce which result?
   a. 1.22220000000000E 004
   b. 12222 DEC(5,0)
   c. 12222 CHAR(5)

5. The data type REAL is a synonym for:
   a. INTEGER
   b. FLOAT
   c. DATE
   d. DOUBLE PRECISION

6. The preferred date format is:
    a. mm/dd/yyyy
    b. dd-mm-yyyy
    c. yy/mm/dd
    d. yyyy/dd/mm
    e. yyyy-mm-dd

7. Internationalization of display formats is controlled by the system's
    a. PDF file.
    b. FDF file.
    c. DSP file.
    d. SDF file.

Chapter Notes

Utilize this space for notes, key points to remember, diagrams, areas of further study, etc.

_____

_____

_____

_____

_____

_____

_____

_____

_____

_____

_____

_____

_____

_____

Chapter 5: Aggregation

Certification Objectives

- ✓ Identify uses involving GROUP BY, HAVING, and DISTINCT.
- ✓ Identify the impact of NULLs on the aggregate functions.
- ✓ Given a scenario, identify which extended GROUP BY operator to use.

Before You Begin

You should be familiar with the following terms and concepts.

Terms	Key Concepts
Aggregations	Identify all the math aggregates and how do they work
Group by	Group By Sets, Rollup, and Cube options
Having	How is this option applied and what does it do

Aggregations

Aggregation functions are used to perform basic arithmetic operations on data values. Aggregate functions can be used together within the same SELECT on either the same or different columns. The following list describes the most common Aggregate functions:

COUNT(*) – Counts all of the rows.

COUNT(*column-name*) – Counts every non null value, within the specified column, and returns the resulting total, as a single value.

SUM(*column-name*) – Sums up all of the values within the specified column and returns the resulting total, as a single value.

AVG(*column-name*) – Sums up all of the values within the specified column and then divides by the count of all rows (provided that the value is not NULL), and returns the average number of all values, as a single value.

MIN(*column-name*) – Compares all values within the specified column and returns the smallest of all the values.

MAX(*column-name*) – Compares all values within the specified column and returns the largest of all the values.

It is important to note that Aggregate functions can only return a <u>single</u> row as the next query demonstrates.

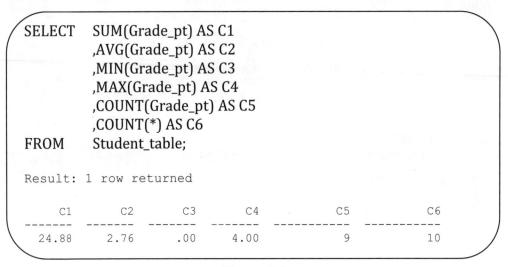

```
SELECT    SUM(Grade_pt) AS C1
          ,AVG(Grade_pt) AS C2
          ,MIN(Grade_pt) AS C3
          ,MAX(Grade_pt) AS C4
          ,COUNT(Grade_pt) AS C5
          ,COUNT(*) AS C6
FROM      Student_table;

Result: 1 row returned

    C1        C2        C3        C4              C5             C6
--------  --------  --------  --------  ------------  ------------
   24.88      2.76       .00      4.00             9            10
```

Figure 5.1

Aggregates Example with Derived Data

The following SELECT sums all employee salaries, provides the average salary, and demonstrates the effect of giving all employees a raise of either 5% or 10%.

```
SELECT    SUM(salary)
          ,SUM(salary*1.05) AS "5% Raise"
          ,SUM(salary*1.10) AS "10% Raise"
          ,AVG(salary)   AS "Avg Salary"
          ,SUM(salary) / COUNT(salary) AS "Computed Avg"
FROM employee_table;

Result: 1 row returned

Sum(Salary)   5% Raise      10% Raise      Avg Salary  Computed Avg
-----------   -----------   -----------    ----------  -----------
421919.38     443015.35     464111.32      46879.93    46879.93
```

Figure 5.2

Using a GROUP BY with Aggregation

Aggregates can only return a single row. In the following query, the first column requests a row for every department number, while the remaining columns can only return a single row.

The following example utilizes the GROUP BY, in order to return the aggregated values, for each department number, within the column.

Think of GROUP BY as *FOR EACH.*

```
SELECT    dept_no  -- For each dept_no, return . . .
          ,SUM(salary) AS SumSal
          ,MAX(salary) AS MaxSal
          ,MIN(salary) AS MinSal
          ,AVG(salary) AS AvgSal
FROM employee_table
GROUP BY dept_no;


Result: 6 rows returned

Dept_No       SumSal        MaxSal        MinSal        AvgSal
-------    ----------    ----------    ----------    ----------
    200      91588.88      48800.00      42788.88      45794.44
      ?      32800.50      32800.50      32800.50      32800.50
    400     144180.00      54590.00      35000.00      48060.00
    100      48850.00      48850.00      48850.00      48850.00
    300      40200.00      40200.00      40200.00      40200.00
     10      64300.00      64300.00      64300.00      64300.00
```

Figure 5.3

If NULL values are allowed, there is potential for the NULL to impact the final outcome of compound tests. Using the IS NOT NULL option is a good technique when NULLs are allowed in a column. However, this does require another comparison and could be written as:

```
SELECT    dept_no  -- For each dept_no, return . . .
          ,SUM(salary) AS SumSal
          ,MAX(salary) AS MaxSal
          ,MIN(salary) AS MinSal
          ,AVG(salary) AS AvgSal
FROM employee_table
GROUP BY dept_no
Where dept_no IS NOT NULL;
```

Figure 5.4

HAVING

HAVING is the "WHERE clause of the GROUP BY" – it is used to limit output values of the GROUP BY. The system first does the GROUP BY and then casts off any groups not matching the HAVING condition.

The following example aggregates all rows, by class code. The result set is restricted to return only those students with a Grade Point Average higher than 3.00.

```
SELECT   Class_code
         ,SUM(Grade_Pt)    AS "Total"
         ,AVG(Grade_Pt)    AS "Average"
         ,COUNT(Grade_Pt) AS "Count"
FROM     student_table
GROUP BY 1
HAVING "Average" > 3.00
ORDER BY 1;

Result: 1 row returned

Class_code    Total  Average        Count
----------    ------ -------    -----------
SR             6.35   3.18              2
```

Figure 5.5

To use a reserved word as a *name*, put it inside double quotes. The quotes become part of the *name*. *Names* can be referenced elsewhere in a query.

GROUP BY ROLLUP

Starting in Teradata 12, the ANSI standard extended grouping functions are supported. These functions allow for aggregations that would normally take multiple queries or unions to produce. Given *n* column references, ROLLUP groups data at *n* levels of detail in one dimension. Doing a ROLLUP on a single column is the same as doing a normal GROUP BY.

The following query produces the normal detail lines, but then adds summary lines for each PID and a grand total.

ROLLUP summarizes on a single dimension only, PID in this example.

```
SELECT Product_id AS PID
     , sale_date
     , SUM(daily_sales) AS Sales
FROM  sales_table
GROUP BY ROLLUP (pid, sale_date)
ORDER BY pid, sale_date
;

Result: 22 rows returned

        PID  Sale_Date          Sales
-----------  ---------  -----------
          ?          ?     869577.35
       1000          ?     346526.72
       1000   07/09/28      45850.40
       1000   07/09/29      64500.22
       1000   07/09/30      36000.07
       1000   07/10/01      45700.43
       1000   07/10/02      33700.50
       1000   07/10/03      66200.00
       1000   07/10/04      54575.10
       2000          ?     302956.81
       2000   07/09/28      42787.88
       2000   07/09/29      46090.00
       2000   07/09/30      44850.03
       2000   07/10/01      58850.29
       2000   07/10/02      35599.93
       2000   07/10/03      41900.18
       2000   07/10/04      32878.50
       3000          ?     220093.82
       3000   07/09/28      60903.77
       3000   07/09/29      34654.13
       3000   07/09/30      42338.86
       3000   07/10/01      27000.00
       3000   07/10/02      18767.94
       3000   07/10/03      21553.79
       3000   07/10/04      14875.33
```

Figure 5.6

GROUP BY GROUPING SETS

Now notice the change when we make the GROUP BY columns GROUPING SETS:

```
SELECT Product_id AS PID
      , sale_date
      , SUM(daily_sales) AS Sales
FROM  sales_table
GROUP BY GROUPING SETS (pid, sale_date)
ORDER BY pid, sale_date
;


Result: 10 rows returned

       PID  Sale_Date        Sales
----------- ---------   -----------
         ?   07/09/28    149542.05
         ?   07/09/29    145244.35
         ?   07/09/30    123188.96
         ?   07/10/01    131550.72
         ?   07/10/02     88068.37
         ?   07/10/03    129653.97
         ?   07/10/04    102328.93
      1000          ?    346526.72
      2000          ?    302956.81
      3000          ?    220093.82
```

Figure 5.7

Notice that we get summary lines for each PID and date.

To get a sales total across all dates and product IDs, add a null column to the GROUPING SETS definition:

```
SELECT Product_id AS PID
      , sale_date
      , SUM(daily_sales) AS Sales
FROM  sales_table
GROUP BY GROUPING SETS (pid, sale_date, ( ) )
ORDER BY pid, sale_date
;


Result: 11 rows returned

        PID  Sale_Date        Sales
----------- ---------- -----------
          ?          ?   869577.35
          ?   07/09/28   149542.05
          ?   07/09/29   145244.35
          ?   07/09/30   123188.96
          ?   07/10/01   131550.72
          ?   07/10/02    88068.37
          ?   07/10/03   129653.97
          ?   07/10/04   102328.93
       1000          ?   346526.72
       2000          ?   302956.81
       3000          ?   220093.82
```

Figure 5.8

In the previous examples, nulls are used to represent an empty set, not missing information. In this case, the nulls mean that information is not reported at the grouping level represented, not that the information is missing from the *sales_table*. The next chart provides a better understanding on how the nulls are utilized.

IF	AND	THEN
PID is null	Sale_date is null	Sales is the sum of all products across all dates
PID is null	Sale_date is not null	Sales is the sum of all products for that date
PID is not null	Sale_date is null	Sales is the sum of that product across all dates.

Figure 5.9

GROUP BY CUBE

CUBE analyzes data by grouping it into multiple dimensions. For *n* dimensions, it creates 2^n groups as illustrated in the next figure. Therefore, each group reports as a single row.

GROUP NUMBER	Dimension 1	Dimension 2
1	X	X
2	X	
3		X
4		

Figure 5.10

The following query has 2 dimensions in the GROUP BY CUBE, which will produce 4 groups in the report.

```
SELECT Product_id AS PID
      , sale_date
      , SUM(daily_sales) AS Sales
FROM  sales_table
GROUP BY CUBE (pid, sale_date)
ORDER BY pid, sale_date ;

Result: 32 rows returned

     PID        Sale_Date         Sales
 -----------    ---------    -----------
       ?            ?         869577.35
       ?         07/09/28     149542.05
       ?         07/09/29     145244.35
       ?         07/09/30     123188.96
       ?         07/10/01     131550.72
       ?         07/10/02      88068.37
       ?         07/10/03     129653.97
       ?         07/10/04     102328.93
      1000           ?        346526.72
      1000        07/09/28     45850.40
      1000        07/09/29     64500.22
      1000        07/09/30     36000.07
      1000        07/10/01     45700.43
      1000        07/10/02     33700.50
      1000        07/10/03     66200.00
      1000        07/10/04     54575.10
      2000           ?        302956.81
      2000        07/09/28     42787.88
      2000        07/09/29     46090.00
      2000        07/09/30     44850.03
      2000        07/10/01     58850.29
      2000        07/10/02     35599.93
      2000        07/10/03     41900.18
      2000        07/10/04     32878.50
      3000           ?        220093.82
      3000        07/09/28     60903.77
      3000        07/09/28     60903.77
      3000        07/09/29     34654.13
      3000        07/09/30     42338.86
      3000        07/10/01     27000.00
      3000        07/10/02     18767.94
      3000        07/10/03     21553.79
      3000        07/10/04     14875.33
```

Figure 5.11

Practice Questions

1. AVG(col_1) and SUM(col_1) / COUNT(*) will produce the same answer even if there are nulls in col_1.
    a. TRUE
    b. FALSE

2. AVG(col_1) and SUM(col_1) / COUNT(col_1) will produce the same answer even if there are nulls in col_1.
    a. TRUE
    b. FALSE

3. SELECT col_3, SUM(col_2) from tbl_1;
    a. Will work as coded.
    b. Will return an error as coded.
    c. Needs GROUP BY col_3 to work.

4. SELECT col_1 AS 'Table' FROM tbl_1; is an example of:
    a. A query that will fail.
    b. Using a reserved word as a *name*.

5. GROUP BY col_1 and GROUP BY ROLLUP col_1 produce the same number of output lines.
    a. TRUE
    b. FALSE

6. Nulls appearing in the output of a grouping set signify missing data.
    a. TRUE
    b. FALSE

7. Grouping functions add summary lines for each group plus a grand total.
   a. TRUE
   b. FALSE

Chapter Notes

Utilize this space for notes, key points to remember, diagrams, areas of further study, etc.

_____

_____

_____

_____

_____

_____

_____

_____

_____

_____

_____

_____

_____

Chapter 6: Subquery Processing

Certification Objectives

- ✓ Given a scenario, identify the SQL statement for a correlated subquery to qualify a subset of data.
- ✓ Given a scenario, identify the SQL statement for a noncorrelated subquery to qualify a subset of data.
- ✓ Given a scenario, identify the use of a derived table.

Before You Begin

You should be familiar with the following terms and concepts.

Terms	Key Concepts
Subquery	How does a subquery work
Table Alias	Understand the reasons for utilizing tables Alias
Correlated Subquery	What are the key differences vs. a standard subquery

Subquery

A Subquery is used to select rows from one table, based on the values from another table. It is a SELECT statement within another SELECT statement that generates a set of values based on an IN or NOT IN list. Therefore, in subquery processing, the lowest level is processed first and those results are input to the next level. This continues until the top level is reached. Lastly, a subquery will always produce a distinct set of values.

The next example utilizes a subquery in order to retrieve all customers with an order exceeding $10,000.

```
SELECT   Customer_name
         ,phone_number
FROM     customer_table
WHERE    customer_number  IN
  ( SELECT  customer_number
    FROM   order_table
    WHERE order_total > 10000 );

Result: 3 rows returned

Customer_name            Phone_number
-------------------      -----------
Best Electronics         559-9987
XYZ Landscapers          447-7954
Database Pros            622-1012
```

Figure 6.1

SUBQUERY using a NOT IN

NOT IN is used when you want to retrieve the rows that do NOT match the specified criteria. This query lists all customers who do not have an order.

```
SELECT  customer_name
       ,phone_number
FROM    customer_table
WHERE  customer_number  NOT IN
       ( SELECT customer_number  FROM order_table) ;

Result: 1 row returned

Customer_name          Phone_number
--------------------   ------------
Acme Designs           555-5564
```

Figure 6.2

SUBQUERY using a NOT IN with NULLs

With NOT IN, there is a potential for including a NULL in the value list, since a NULL will compare either a False or UNKNOWN.

```
SELECT  customer_name
        ,phone_number
FROM    customer_table
WHERE customer_number  NOT IN
        ( SELECT customer_number
          FROM   order_table
          WHERE customer_number IS NOT NULL) ;

Result: 1 row returned

Customer_name          Phone_number
-------------------    ------------
Acme Designs           555-5564
```

Figure 6.3

Note: The NOT IN has the potential for a NULL to be returned in the result set. It is recommended to code an IS NOT NULL compound comparison to remove the NULLs.

Correlated Subquery Processing

The second type of subquery is a correlated subquery. Correlated subqueries differ for traditional subqueries because each row from the outer query is retrieved and compared to the criteria in the subquery. These types of queries are often used when the basis of comparison is an aggregate value from the same table.

The following query returns the highest paid employee, by department. Notice the word "AS", which is used to alias the table name. Table aliasing is described in more detail in Chapter 7.

```
SELECT  last_name
       , first_name
       , dept_no
       , salary
FROM    employee_table  AS emp
WHERE  salary =
       ( SELECT MAX(salary)
         FROM employee_table  AS emt
         WHERE  emp.dept_no = emt.dept_no )
ORDER BY 3,1 ;

Result: 6 rows returned

Last_name              First_name    Dept_No      Salary
--------------------   -----------   -------   ----------
Gere                   Richard            10    64300.00
Student                Mandee            100    48850.00
Roberts                Julia             200    48800.00
Mcfly                  Loraine           300    40200.00
Ford                   Harrison          400    54590.00
Strickland             Stan              400    54590.00
```

Figure 6.4

Subquery Processing with Derived tables

The third subquery processing type is the derived table. A derived table is a temporary table that is named, getting its results from a subquery. These tables are created in the user's spool space, can be used in other parts of the query and are deleted when the query finishes.

This derived table example shows the employees whose salary is greater than their department average.

```
SELECT  last_name AS LAST
       ,salary        (FORMAT '$,$$$,$99.99') AS sal
       ,dept_no       AS dep
       ,avgsal        (FORMAT '$,$$$,$99.99') FROM
       (SELECT AVG (salary)
              ,dept_no
       FROM  employee_table
       GROUP BY dept_no)
       my_temp (avgsal, deptno)
       , employee_table
WHERE deptno = dept_no AND sal > avgsal
ORDER BY 2 DESC;


Result: 3 rows returned

LAST                          sal     dep        avgsal
--------------------   -----------   ------   ------------
Ford                    $54,590.00    400     $48,060.00
Strickland              $54,590.00    400     $48,060.00
Roberts                 $48,800.00    200     $45,794.44
```

Figure 6.5

Practice Questions

1. Which query will return the correct answer if col_3 has nulls?
    a. SELECT col_1, col_2 FROM t_1
       WHERE col_1 NOT IN
       (SELECT col_3 FROM t_2);
    b. SELECT col_1, col_2 FROM t_1
       WHERE col_1 NOT IN
       (SELECT col_3 FROM t_2
         WHERE col_3 IS NOT NULL);

2. The differences between a traditional subquery and a correlated subquery are:
    a. A traditional subquery is used to select rows from one table based upon the values from another table.
    b. A traditional subquery compares the rows of the outer query to the rows of the inner query.
    c. A correlated subquery specifies a comparison between the outer and inner queries.
    d. A correlated subquery is used to select rows from one table based upon the values from another table.

3. The space for derived tables comes from the user's permanent space.
    a. TRUE
    b. FALSE

4. Derived tables are automatically dropped at the end of a query.
    a. TRUE
    b. FALSE

5. A derived table is declared in the WHERE clause of a query.
    a. TRUE
    b. FALSE

Chapter Notes

Utilize this space for notes, key points to remember, diagrams, areas of further study, etc.

_____

_____

_____

_____

_____

_____

_____

_____

_____

_____

_____

_____

_____

_____

Teradata 12 Certification Study Guide

Chapter 7: Join Processing

Certification Objectives

- ✓ Given a scenario, determine the type of join to code in order to get the desired result set.
- ✓ Identify proper and improper use of aliasing in table joins.
- ✓ Given a scenario, identify the evaluation order of various join types.
- ✓ Given a scenario with two partitioned tables, identify the correct way to join them.

Before You Begin

You should be familiar with the following terms and concepts.

Terms	Key Concepts
Inner Join	Syntax of an INNER JOIN
Outer Join	OUTER JOIN SQL and how they process
Product Joins	What to look for with a PRODUCT JOIN
Residuals	PPI, and Where clause considerations with JOINs

Table Aliasing

An alias is user-specified, temporary name given to a table, within the SQL. Aliases are useful for shortening long table names, especially when a table is reference multiple times in the SQL.

Syntax:
SELECT * FROM <table name>   AS <table alias name>;

The alias is simply a reference to an existing table name - the real table name is not changed. Use double quotes " " around alias name when using spaces or SQL keywords in the alias. The keyword "AS" is optional.

Join Processing

A JOIN occurs when two or more tables are linked together within the same SELECT statement. Tables are joined together using one or more columns that create a common domain between the tables. Joins can be performed on either equality or inequality comparison but are usually used for equal comparisons. Like in a single table SELECT, each table is listed following the FROM clause.

The objective of an INNER JOIN is to return the matching rows between two or more tables.

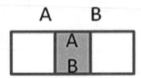

INNER JOIN

The next example uses an INNER JOIN to find all customers with valid orders based on the common column (or domain) they share, customer number.

```
SELECT   cust.customer_number AS Cust_no
         ,cust.customer_name
         ,ord.order_number
         ,ord.order_total
FROM     customer_table AS cust
INNER JOIN
         order_table AS ord
ON       cust.customer_number = ord.customer_number
ORDER BY 2 ;

Result: 6 rows returned

    Cust_no  Customer_name     Order_Number    Order_Total
-----------  ----------------  ------------    -----------
   31323134  ABC Consulting          123552        5311.47
   31323134  ABC Consulting          999999              ?
   11111111  Best Electronics        123512        7995.91
   11111111  Best Electronics        123456       12447.53
   87323456  Database Pros           123585       16231.62
   57896883  XYZ Landscapers         123777       25454.84
```

Figure 7.1

INNER JOIN - Three Table Example using AND Clause

The following query is a three table INNER JOIN that finds all students enrolled in a 'SQL' course. The common column(s) (or domain) between the tables being joined in the ON clauses are the student_id and course_id.

```
SELECT    s.last_name AS "Last Name"
          ,CAST(s.student_id AS CHAR(6))
          ,CAST(c.course_name AS CHAR(20)) AS Course
FROM      Student_table AS s
INNER JOIN
          student_course_table AS sc
ON        s.student_id = sc.student_id
INNER JOIN
          course_table AS c
ON        c.course_id = sc.course_id
AND       course_name LIKE '%SQL%'
ORDER BY course, last_name;


Result: 7 rows returned

Last Name               Student_ID   Course
-------------------     ----------   --------------------
McCormick               231222       Advanced SQL
Rieter                  280023       Advanced SQL
Craig                   324652       Introduction to SQL
Kojack                  125634       Introduction to SQL
Bond                    322133       TD12 SQL Features
Kojack                  125634       TD12 SQL Features
McCormick               231222       TD12 SQL Features
```

Figure 7.2

OUTER JOIN

An OUTER JOIN returns all rows from the Outer Table and the rows from the INNER table based on the join condition. OUTER JOINs are useful because they show the rows that match as well as the rows that don't. There are three types of OUTER JOINs:

left_table **LEFT OUTER JOIN** *right_table* – left table is the outer table. All rows from the left table will be in the result set.

left_table **RIGHT OUTER JOIN** *right_table* – right table is the outer table. All rows from the right table will be in the result set.

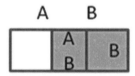

left_table **FULL OUTER JOIN** *right_table* – both are outer tables. All rows from both the left and right tables will be in the result set.

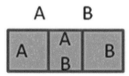

The next series of pages illustrate specific examples that emphasize the points above.

LEFT OUTER JOIN

The following example returns customers with orders along with those who have NOT placed an order. This helps to identify the non-buying customers. It also shows how to use aliases.

```
SELECT  cust.customer_name
        ,ord.order_number
        ,ord.order_total
FROM    customer_table cust
LEFT OUTER JOIN
        order_table ord
ON      cust.customer_number = ord.customer_number
ORDER BY 1;


Result: 7 rows returned

Customer_name         Order_Number    Order_Total
--------------------  ------------    ------------
ABC Consulting            123552         5311.47
Acme Designs                   ?               ?
Best Electronics          123456        12447.53
Best Electronics          123512         7995.91
Database Pros             123585        16231.62
XYZ Landscapers           123777        25454.84
```

Figure 7.3

RIGHT OUTER JOIN

All rows from the right table – order table - will be in the result set. The query below returns orders with matching customers along with those orders who do NOT have customers. This helps to identify incorrect orders.

```
SELECT   cust.customer_name
         ,ord.order_number
         ,ord.order_total
FROM     customer_table cust
RIGHT OUTER JOIN
         order_table ord
ON       cust.customer_number = ord.customer_number
ORDER BY 1 ;

Result: 6 rows returned

Customer_name          Order_Number    Order_Total
--------------------   ------------    ------------
?                            999999               ?
ABC Consulting               123552         5311.47
Best Electronics             123512         7995.91
Best Electronics             123456        12447.53
Database Pros                123585        16231.62
XYZ Landscapers              123777        25454.84
```

Figure 7.4

FULL OUTER JOIN

All rows from both the left and right tables will be in the result set. The following example uses a FULL OUTER JOIN to return all customers with orders, orders without customers, and customers without orders.

```
SELECT  cust.customer_name
        ,ord.order_number
        ,ord.order_total
FROM    customer_table cust
FULL OUTER JOIN
        order_table  ord
ON      cust.customer_number = ord.customer_number
ORDER BY 1 ;


Result: 7 rows returned

Customer_name           Order_Number    Order_Total
--------------------    ------------    ------------
?                             999999               ?
ABC Consulting               123552         5311.47
Acme Designs                      ?               ?
Best Electronics             123456        12447.53
Best Electronics             123512         7995.91
Database Pros                123585        16231.62
XYZ Landscapers              123777        25454.84
```

Figure 7.5

Residual Conditions

Including a WHERE clause adds residual conditions to be applied to the joined rows. The following eliminates the two rows that have a null for the course name:

```
SELECT  s.student_id
        ,sc.course_id
        ,c.course_name
FROM   student_table AS s
FULL OUTER JOIN
        student_course_table AS sc
ON     s.student_id = sc.student_id
FULL OUTER JOIN
        course_table  AS c
ON     c.course_id = sc.course_id
WHERE course_name IS NOT NULL
ORDER BY 2;


Result: 14 rows returned

 Student_ID  Course_ID  Course_name
-----------  ---------  -------------------------------
     234121        100  Teradata Basics
     123250        100  Teradata Basics
     125634        100  Teradata Basics
     324652        200  Introduction to SQL
     125634        200  Introduction to SQL
     231222        210  Advanced SQL
     280023        210  Advanced SQL
     231222        220  TD12 SQL Features
     125634        220  TD12 SQL Features
     322133        220  TD12 SQL Features
     322133        300  Physical Database Tuning
     333450        400  Database Administration
     260000        400  Database Administration
```

Figure 7.6

The following rules and recommendations apply to coding ON and WHERE clauses for outer joins:

1. One or more join conditions, or connecting terms, are required in the ON clause for each table in an outer join. These join conditions define the rows in the outer table that take part in the match to the inner table.

2. The best practice is to use *only* join conditions in ON clauses. However, when a search condition is applied to the *inner* table in a WHERE clause, it should be applied in the ON clause. A search condition in the ON clause of the inner table does *not* limit the number of rows in the answer set. Instead, it defines the rows that are eligible to take part in the match to the outer table.

3. An outer join can also include a WHERE clause; however, the results you get with a WHERE clause may be surprising and not obvious or even intuitive. To limit the number of qualifying rows in the outer table (and therefore the answer set), the search condition for the outer table must be in the WHERE clause. Note that the Optimizer *logically* applies the WHERE clause condition only after a join has been produced. The *actual* application of conditions always depends on how the Optimizer chooses to implement the query.

4. If a search condition on the inner table is placed in the WHERE clause, the join is logically equivalent to an inner join, even if you explicitly specify the keywords LEFT/RIGHT/FULL OUTER JOIN in the query. The Optimizer always treats such a join as an inner join to simplify the query, rewriting it to roll the entire complex process into a single step.

Evaluation Order

The result of an inner join of two tables does not change if rows from one table are joined to rows from another. This is because inner joins are both commutative and associative. Therefore, the Optimizer can select the best join order and the end result is always the same.

Outer joins however, are rarely commutative or associative. In this case, the Optimizer cannot select the best join order for outer joins because it does not have any way of knowing the specific result that was intended with the query.

Given the above, if you have a three table outer join, then you must specify their join order explicitly by placing the ON clause in an appropriate position within the FROM clause to ensure that the join is evaluated correctly. The Optimizer adheres to the following rules when generating join orders for outer joins:

- The first ON clause in the query - reading from left to right - is evaluated first.
- Any ON clause applies to its immediately preceding join operation.

Self-Join

The following example joins the Employee table to itself in order to find all of the managers (not all employees are managers). In addition, the Department table is joined in order to return each manager's department information.

```
SELECT   mgr.employee_no  AS "Manager Number"
         , mgr.last_name      AS "Manager Name"
         , dept.dept_no
FROM     employee_table AS Emp
INNER JOIN
         employee_table  AS Mgr
ON       mgr.employee_no = emp.mgr_employee_no
INNER JOIN
         department_table  AS Dept
ON       mgr.dept_no = dept.dept_no
ORDER BY 2 ;


Result: 7 rows returned

Manager Number   Manager Name              Dept_No
--------------   --------------------      -------
       1256349   Ford                          400
       1256349   Ford                          400
       1333454   Roberts                       200
       1333454   Roberts                       200
       1121334   Strickland                    400
       1121334   Strickland                    400
       1121334   Strickland                    400
```

Figure 7.7

Cross Join

A CROSS JOIN takes <u>every</u> row from the left table and joins it to <u>every</u> row in the right table. The following example demonstrates a CROSS JOIN that introduces a WHERE clause to retrieve a specific course_id and then joins it to every row in the student_table.

```
SELECT  course_name
        ,student_id
FROM    student_table
CROSS JOIN
        course_table
WHERE Course_ID  = 100 ;


Result: 10 rows returned

Course_name                          Student_ID
-------------------------------      -----------
Teradata Basics                          423400
Teradata Basics                          231222
Teradata Basics                          280023
Teradata Basics                          322133
Teradata Basics                          125634
Teradata Basics                          333450
Teradata Basics                          324652
Teradata Basics                          260000
Teradata Basics                          234121
Teradata Basics                          123250
```

Figure 7.8

Note: Not all students listed are enrolled in this class.

Cross Join - Continued

The following example uses a WHERE clause to limit the rows for the customer "Best Electronics" and associate the result with <u>every</u> row in the Order Table. This type of join can have a major impact on system performance and is normally avoided.

```
SELECT  customer_name
        ,order_number
        ,order_total
FROM    customer_table  AS cust
        ,order_table    AS ord
WHERE   customer_name = 'Best Electronics';


Result: 6 rows returned

Customer_name            Order_Number    Order_Total
-------------------      ------------    ------------
Best Electronics               999999               ?
Best Electronics               123777        25454.84
Best Electronics               123585        16231.62
Best Electronics               123456        12447.53
Best Electronics               123512         7995.91
Best Electronics               123552         5311.47
```

Figure 7.9

Note: Product Joins can be prohibited on a user / group basis.

Join Consideration and PPI

Teradata has made the optimizer aware of join operations that would occur between PI and PPI tables. This merge join might be slightly slower than a traditional PI merge join. However, if you have a solid partition elimination strategy on the PPI table, then performance should be equal to that of a traditional merge join.

The Optimizer has (3) methods when joining PPI to non-PPI (NPPI) tables, and when joining two PPI tables that have different partition columns defined. These are as follows:

1. When joining two PPI tables that have different partition columns, the Optimizer could choose to spool one or both of the PPI tables in order to convert it to a NPPI table(s) in spool and then complete the merge join.

2. When joining an NPPI with a PPI table, the optimizer may opt to spool the non-PPI table and convert it into a PPI table in spool. This approach would create the new PPI table in spool with the same partition strategy as the base PPI table which will enable the join to complete on a RowID merge join.

3. When joining NPPI and PPI tables that have the same Primary Index (PI), the optimizer can match the rows based on the PI. From there, the optimizer can determine how many partitions are required from the PPI table to complete the join. In this case, spool will not be utilized to complete the join operation.

Finally, it is important to make sure statistics are collected on the primary indexes, the partition columns in the PPI table and on the columns in the NPPI table that are the same as the partition column in the PPI table.

Practice Questions

1. Product joins can be prohibited on a user/group basis.
    a. TRUE
    b. FALSE

2. The join order for Outer joins is the same as the join order for inner joins.
    a. TRUE
    b. FALSE

3. The best practice is to put join conditions and search conditions in the ON clauses.
    a. TRUE
    b. FALSE

4. FROM mylongtablename, t2 WHERE mylongtablename.col1 = t2.col1 and FROM mylongtablename JOIN t2 ON mylongtablename.col1 = t2.col1 are functionally equivalent.
    a. TRUE
    b. FALSE

5. Which of the following are correct?
    a. SELECT * FROM mylongtablename t
    b. SELECT * FROM mylongtablename AS t
    c. SELECT * FROM mylongtablename TITLE 't'
    d. SELECT * FROM mylongtablename "table 1"

6. Which of the following statements are TRUE when joining PPI and NPPI tables?
    a. Collect statistics on the primary indexes of both tables.
    b. Collect statistics on the partition columns of the PPI table.
    c. Collect statistics on the NPPI columns that match the PPI partition columns.
    d. All of the above.
    e. None of the above.

Chapter Notes

Utilize this space for notes, key points to remember, diagrams, areas of further study, etc.

_____

_____

_____

_____

_____

_____

_____

_____

_____

_____

_____

_____

_____

_____

Chapter 8: Date and Time Processing

Certification Objectives

- ✓ Identify the correct use of Time/Date in expressions involving computations, conversions, literals, and extractions.
- ✓ Identify the correct use of Timestamp in expressions involving computations, conversions, literals, and extractions.
- ✓ Identify the correct use of Intervals in expressions involving computations, conversions, literals, date intervals, and extractions.
- ✓ Given a date, identify valid date calculations in a Teradata database.

Before You Begin

You should be familiar with the following terms and concepts.

Terms	Key Concepts
Date Forms	Differences with ANSI vs. Teradata dates
Date Processing	Methods for processing dates
Time	Timestamp data type options and SQL operations with time
Intervals	Arithmetic and casting options

Temporal Data Types

In an earlier chapter, you were introduced to the temporal data types which allow you to store date, time, and time-interval information. These allow you to deal with past/present/future events.

The figure below reviews the temporal data types that are supported.

Date/Time	Description
DATE	Special type of integer. ((YEAR - 1900) * 10000) + (MONTH * 100) + DAY Use ANSI Date form for compatibility. 4 bytes
TIME (n)	Stored as HHMMSS.nnnnnn 6 bytes
TIMESTAMP (n)	Stored as YYMMDDHHMMSS.nnnnnn 10 bytes
TIME (n) WITH ZONE	Stored as HHMMSS.nnnnnn+HHMM 8 bytes
TIMESTAMP (n) WITH ZONE	Stored as YYMMDDHHMMSS.nnnnnn+HHMM 12 bytes

Figure 8.1

Temporal Functions

Though portions of dates can be accessed using standard integer arithmetic, Teradata provides the following functions to make handling temporal values easier.

Function	Description
ADD_MONTHS (d, n)	The function returns the date d plus the n months. You can use any integer for n months. If d is the last day of the month, or if the resulting month has fewer days than the day component, then the result is the last day of the resulting month. Otherwise, the result has the same day component as d.

EXTRACT (*period* FROM *value*)	PERIOD	SPECIFIES...
	YEAR	that the integer value for YEAR is to be extracted from the date represented by *value*.
	MONTH	that the integer value for MONTH is to be extracted from the date represented by *value*.
	DAY	that the integer value for DAY is to be extracted from the date represented by *value*.
	HOUR	that the integer value for HOUR is to be extracted from the time represented by *value*.
	MINUTE	that the integer value for MINUTE is to be extracted from the time represented by *value*.
	SECOND	that the integer value for SECOND is to be extracted from the time represented by *value*.
	TIMEZONE_HOUR	that the integer value for TIMEZONE_HOUR is to be extracted from the time represented by *value*.
	TIMEZONE_MINUTE	that the integer value for TIMEZONE_MINUTE is to be extracted from the time represented by *value*.

| (d1) OVERLAPS (d2) | The function determines if two time intervals overlap. Teradata SQL supports the standard SQL overlaps predicate.
Each time period to the left and right of the OVERLAPS keyword is one of the following expression types:
• DateTime, DateTime
• DateTime, Interval
• Row subquery |

Figure 8.2

DATEFORM

The display of DATE values is supported both in its Teradata form and the ANSI DateTime form. Though date values are stored as an integer, the default display of date values is controlled by the system parameter *Current DateForm.* This parameter is set by the system administrator.

DATE data can be set to be treated either using the ANSI date format (DATEFORM=ANSIDATE) or using the Teradata date format (DATEFORM=INTEGERDATE).

The following table explains the differences.

Option	Description
INTEGERDATE	Sets the DATEFORM option to import and export DATE values as encoded integers. INTEGERDATE results in a default DATE format in field mode of 'YY/MM/DD' for date columns created and for date constants in character form. INTEGERDATE is the default.

ANSIDATE	Sets the DATEFORM option to import and export DATE values as CHARACTER(10). Results in a 'YYYY-MM-DD' date format for date columns created and for date constants in character form.

Figure 8.3

You can see the setting of this parameter through the HELP SESSION; command.

Date Arithmetic

As mentioned earlier, dates are stored internally in an INTEGER as ((YEAR - 1900) * 10000) + (MONTH * 100) + DAY

Here are some examples of the Teradata DATE:

July 4, 1776 = (1776 -1900) * 10000 + 07 * 100 + 04 = -1240704
January 1, 2000 = (2000 – 1900) * 10000 + 01 * 100 + 01 = 1000101

Here is an example:

```
SELECT CURRENT_DATE, CAST(CURRENT_DATE AS INTEGER);

Result: 1 row returned

    Date           Date
 --------     -----------
10/08/26        1100826
```

Figure 8.4

Note: Please see Figure 8.3 for more information regarding the above examples.

Because Teradata stores dates as an integer data type, arithmetic operations can be used to extract portions of dates as shown in this figure:

```
SELECT CAST(CURRENT_DATE AS INTEGER) AS INT_Date
     , CURRENT_DATE / 10000 + 1900 AS "Year"
     , CURRENT_DATE / 100 MOD 100 AS "Month"
     , CURRENT_DATE MOD 100 AS "Day"
;

Result: 1 row returned

   INT_Date          Year         Month          Day
----------    ----------   ----------    ----------
   1100826          2010             8           26
```

Figure 8.5

When doing addition and subtraction on dates, the system converts the dates to a linear number of days, does the math, and then converts the result back to a calendar date.

EXTRACT

To EXTRACT function retrieves portions of date and time, such as year or hour, from DATE, TIME, or TIMESTAMP values. The following example illustrates this.

```
SELECT CURRENT_TIMESTAMP
, EXTRACT(YEAR FROM CURRENT_DATE)   AS Yr_Part
, EXTRACT(MONTH FROM CURRENT_DATE) AS Mth_Part
, EXTRACT(DAY FROM CURRENT_TIMESTAMP)   AS Day_Part
, EXTRACT(HOUR FROM CURRENT_TIMESTAMP)   AS Hr_Part
, EXTRACT(MINUTE FROM CURRENT_TIME) AS Min_Part
, EXTRACT(SECOND FROM CURRENT_TIME) AS Sec_Part
,EXTRACT(TIMEZONE_HOUR FROM CURRENT_TIMESTAMP)AS TZ_Hr
,EXTRACT(TIMEZONE_MINUTE FROM CURRENT_TIMESTAMP) AS
TZ_Min ;

Result: 1 row returned

Current  TimeStamp(6)    2010-07-26 08:33:14.140000+00:00
            Yr_Part            2010
           Mth_Part               7
           Day_Part              26
            Hr_Part               8
           Min_Part              33
           Sec_Part              14
             TZ_Hr               0
            TZ_Min               0
```

Figure 8.6

EXTRACT with Aggregates

The following example will display the selling month along with how many of each product was sold and their average for the month.

```
SELECT  product_id
        , EXTRACT(MONTH FROM sale_date) AS Sale_month
        ,AVG(daily_sales) AS Avg_sale
        , COUNT(*) AS Sales_count
FROM   sales_table
GROUP BY 1,2
ORDER BY 2,3 ;
```

The same query using date arithmetic:

```
SELECT  product_id
        , sale_date /100 MOD 100 AS Sale_month
        ,AVG(daily_sales) AS Avg_sale
        , COUNT(*) AS Sales_count
FROM   sales_table
GROUP BY 1,2
ORDER BY 2,3 ;
```

```
Result: 6 rows returned

 Product_ID    Sale_month      Avg_sale   Sales_count
 -----------   -----------   -----------  -----------
       2000             9     44575.97             3
       3000             9     45965.59             3
       1000             9     48783.56             3
       3000            10     20549.26             4
       2000            10     42307.22             4
       1000            10     50044.01             4
```

Figure 8.7

Though both queries produced the desired report, the first one, using the EXTRACT, is easier to understand.

Date and Time Literals

Teradata SQL is written to handle date literals in either the Teradata format ('yy/mm/dd') or the ANSI format ('yyyy-mm-dd').

The way to specify a date literal value with the ANSI date literal form is 'yyyy-mm-dd'. A valid ANSI date literal requires no additional format validation for SQL date operations.

Regardless of the Transaction mode (BTET, ANSI), the following query will execute because the literal is in ANSI format.

```
SELECT CAST('2002-11-21' AS DATE);

Result: 1 row returned

'2002-11-21'
------------
   02/11/21
```

Figure 8.8

This query will also execute, regardless of the Transaction mode (BTET, ANSI), because the literal matches the Teradata default for dates.

```
SELECT CAST('02/11/21' AS DATE);

Result: 1 row returned

'02/11/21'
----------
   02/11/21
```

Figure 8.9

Without a FORMAT clause, the following query will fail since the literal does not match either the ANSI or Teradata format.

```
SELECT CAST('Nov 21, 2002' AS DATE);

*** Failure 2665 Invalid date.
              Statement# 1, Info =0
```

Figure 8.10

You can use a FORMAT clause to tell the system how to interpret a non-standard date value as shown below.

```
SELECT CAST('Nov 21, 2002' AS DATE FORMAT 'MMMbDD,bYYYY');

Result: 1 row returned

'Nov 21, 2002'
--------------
  Nov 21, 2002
```

Figure 8.11

The following example will change the order_date for one row in the order_table using a non-standard date format.

```
UPDATE order_table
SET order_date =
CAST('21/2002/11' AS DATE FORMAT 'dd/y4/mm')
WHERE order_number = 123777;

*** Update completed. One row changed.

SELECT *
FROM order_table
WHERE order_number = 123777;

Result: 1 row returned

Order_Number   Customer_number   Order_Date    Order_Total
------------   ---------------   ----------    ------------
      123777          57896883    02/11/21        25454.84
```

Figure 8.12

The following SQL will change the order_date back to its original value. Notice how much cleaner the SQL is when a standard format is used for the date value.

```
UPDATE order_table
SET order_date = '2007-09-09'
WHERE order_number = 123777;

*** Update completed. One row changed.

SELECT *
FROM order_table
WHERE order_number = 123777;

Result: 1 row returned

Order_Number   Customer_number   Order_Date    Order_Total
------------   ---------------   ----------    ------------
      123777          57896883     07/09/09        25454.84
```

Figure 8.13

INTERVAL Processing

In creating an Interval clause, it is important to remember that the literal string can only be interpreted in the context of the interval type where it is explicitly declared. In other words INTERVAL '30' is ambiguous because it could imply 30 years, 30 months, or 30 days.

In the following example, notice how the system adjusts for the length of the months involved.

```
SELECT  product_id
       , sale_date
       , sale_date + INTERVAL '30' DAY AS Due_Date
       , sale_date + INTERVAL '20' DAY AS Discount_Date
FROM   sales_table
WHERE product_id = 1000;


Result: 7 rows returned

 Product_ID  Sale_Date  Due_Date  Discount_Date
-----------  ---------  --------  -------------
       1000  07/09/28   07/10/28       07/10/18
       1000  07/09/29   07/10/29       07/10/19
       1000  07/09/30   07/10/30       07/10/20
       1000  07/10/01   07/10/31       07/10/21
       1000  07/10/02   07/11/01       07/10/22
       1000  07/10/03   07/11/02       07/10/23
       1000  07/10/04   07/11/03       07/10/24
```

Figure 8.14

As seen above in Figure 8.14, the literal value for an interval goes inside of quote marks. Any arithmetic operator is placed outside the leading quote mark. As an example: INTERVAL –'30' DAY

In the INTERVAL YEAR TO MONTH example below, the system interprets the literal '3-07' as a number of years (3) and a number of months (07).

```
SELECT (INTERVAL '3-07'  YEAR TO MONTH) * 4;

Result: 1 row returned

( 3-07*4)
---------
   14-04
```

This is the equivalent of:
SELECT (((3*12) + 7)*4)/12 , (((3*12) + 7)*4) MOD 12

Figure 8.15

Note: 3 years 7 months = 43 months

43 * 4 = 172 months

172 months /12 = 14 years 4 months

Suppose you want to know how much time elapsed between a start time and an ending time. This is shown in the example below.

```
SELECT call_et, call_st, (call_et - call_st) SECOND(4)
FROM phcall
WHERE area_code = 650 AND phone_no = 5601140;

Result: 1 row returned

call_et       call_st      (call_et - call_st) SECOND
2006-01-23 09:00:06   2006-01-23 08:49:41 625.000000
```

Figure 8.16

You can use CAST to convert one interval type to another interval type. The only requirement is that both types must belong to the same Interval group, either the Year-Month or Day-Time group.

The following example converts a DAY TO SECOND interval to a given number of hours.

```
SELECT CAST(INTERVAL '135 12:37:25.26' DAY TO SECOND AS
INTERVAL HOUR(4));

Result: 1 row returned

 135 12:37:25.26
---------------
           3252
```

Figure 8.17

OVERLAPS

The OVERLAP function is used to test whether two time periods overlap one another. It returns either TRUE or FALSE.

Each side of the OVERLAPS must specify a starting and ending point in time.

The following query will not return a row since the two time spans DO NOT overlap. They meet at CURRENT_TIME(0).

```
SELECT 'OVERLAPS'
WHERE (CURRENT_TIME(0), INTERVAL '1' HOUR)
OVERLAPS (CURRENT_TIME(0), INTERVAL -'1' HOUR);
```

Figure 8.18

This query will return a row since the time periods overlap by one second.

```
SELECT 'OVERLAPS'
WHERE (CURRENT_TIME(0), INTERVAL '1' HOUR) OVERLAPS
 (CURRENT_TIME(0) + INTERVAL '1' SECOND, INTERVAL -'1' HOUR);

Result: 1 row returned

'OVERLAPS'
----------
OVERLAPS
```

Figure 8.19

This query will also return a row.

```
SELECT 'OVERLAPS'
WHERE (DATE '2000-01-15', DATE '2002-12-15')
OVERLAPS (DATE '2001-06-15', DATE '2005-06-15');

Result: 1 row returned

'OVERLAPS'
----------
OVERLAPS
```

Figure 8.20

Practice Questions

1. Which of the following is correct?
    a. INTERVAL -'5' HOUR
    b. INTERVAL '-5' HOUR

2. What answer will this query return?
   SELECT CAST(INTERVAL '20' DAY AS INTERVAL HOUR(4));
    a. 480
    b. 240
    c. Error
    d. None of the above.

3. Which of the following is not a valid interval data type?
    a. INTERVAL YEAR TO MONTH
    b. INTERVAL MONTH TO DAY
    c. INTERVAL DAY TO HOUR
    d. INTERVAL HOUR TO MINUTE
    e. INTERVAL MINUTE TO SECOND

4. Which of the following is equivalent to EXTRACT (MONTH FROM CURRENT_DATE)?
    a. CURRENT_DATE / 10000
    b. CURRENT_DATE / 100 MOD 100
    c. CURRENT_DATE MOD 100

5. A row subquery can be used with the OVERLAPS function.
    a. TRUE
    b. FALSE

6. Year-Month and Day-Time are the two interval groups.
    a. TRUE
    b. FALSE

Chapter Notes

Utilize this space for notes, key points to remember, diagrams, areas of further study, etc.

Teradata 12 Certification Study Guide

Chapter 9: Character String Processing

Certification Objectives

- ✓ Identify the attribute functions and identify how they work within SQL.
- ✓ Identify the correct use of string manipulation functions and attributes.

Before You Begin

You should be familiar with the following terms and concepts.

Terms	Key Concepts
Character Data	Functions used to transform character data
Trim	How to apply along with understand the options
Substring	When to use properly
Concatenation	Utilizing SQL to combine column fields

Teradata SQL provides many ways to manipulate character data. Most of the ways are ANSI standard, while a few are Teradata extensions.

The following chart summarizes your choices:

IF you want to ...	THEN use ...
Concatenate strings	Concatenation character ||
Get the starting position of a substring within another string	POSITION or INDEX INDEX is a Teradata extension

Convert a character string to lowercase	LOWER
Convert a character string to uppercase	UPPER Note: This is a Teradata extension
Extract a substring from another string	SUBSTRING or SUBSTR SUBSTR is a Teradata extension
Trim specified pad characters or bytes from a character or byte string	TRIM
Count the number of characters in a string	CHARACTER_LENGTH is a synonym for the Teradata CHARACTERS function
Count the number of bytes in a byte string	BYTES Note: This is a Teradata extension
See the default value assigned to a column in the CREATE TABLE	SELECT DEFAULT(*columnname*) This is a Teradata extension
See the display format assigned to a column in the CREATE TABLE	SELECT FORMAT(*columnname*) This is a Teradata extension

Figure 9.1

TRIM

Though VARCHAR will automatically trim trailing blanks, it will not trim leading blanks. VARBYTE will automatically trim trailing bytes of binary 00 but not leading bytes of binary 00.

Most frequently, TRIM is used on fixed-length data along with concatenation.

The following example shows the variations of a TRIM.

```
SELECT '**1234**'
      , TRIM(LEADING '*' FROM '**1234**')
      , TRIM(TRAILING '*' FROM '**1234**')
      , TRIM(BOTH '*' FROM '**1234**');

Result: 1 row returned

                            '**1234**'   **1234**
 Trim(LEADING '*' FROM '**1234**')   1234**
Trim(TRAILING '*' FROM '**1234**')   **1234
    Trim(BOTH '*' FROM '**1234**')   1234
```

Figure 9.2

Implicit Data Conversion

The TRIM function is designed to operate on character data. If numeric data is supplied, it will be converted to character data first.

The following is an example where the literal supplied is numeric.

```
SELECT employee_no
    ,TRIM(LEADING 0 FROM employee_no)
FROM  employee_table;

*** Failure 5388 The Pad Expression for TRIM has an
incorrect data type or length.
```

Figure 9.3

In this next example, the literal has been changed to alphanumeric to match the implicit numeric to character conversion of the input.

```
SELECT employee_no
    ,TRIM(LEADING '0' FROM employee_no)
FROM  employee_table;

Result: 9 rows returned

Employee_No   Trim(LEADING '0' FROM Employee_No)
-----------   ---------------------------------
    2000000       2000000
    1333454       1333454
    1000234       1000234
    1256349       1256349
    1232578       1232578
    1121334       1121334
    2341218       2341218
    1324657       1324657
    2312225       2312225
```

Figure 9.4

TRIM and Concatenation

As mention above, TRIM is frequently combined with concatenation. The following example shows two ways of displaying names.

```
SELECT TRIM(last_name) || ',' || first_name AS Example1
      ,first_name || ' ' || TRIM(last_name) AS Example2
FROM   employee_table
ORDER BY 1;

Result: 9 rows returned

Example1                              Example2
---------------------------------     ---------------------------------
Clooney, George                       George
Clooney
Ford, Harrison                        Harrison Ford
Gere, Richard                         Richard Gere
Mcfly, Loraine                        Loraine Mcfly
Roberts, Julia                        Julia Roberts
Strickland, Stan                      Stan Strickland
Student, Mandee                       Mandee Student
Travolta, John                        John Travolta
Willis, Bruce                         Bruce Willis
```

Figure 9.5

The *first_name* column is VARCHAR and does not need to be trimmed.

CHARACTER_LENGTH and CHARACTERS Functions

The CHARACTER_LENGTH (ANSI) and the CHARACTERS (Teradata) functions are only meaningful with VARCHAR and VARBYTE data. They return the length of a string as a count of logical characters or bytes.

You can use the TRIM function to transform a fixed length string into a variable length string, as shown below.

```
SELECT last_name
     , CHARACTERS(last_name)
     , CHARACTER_LENGTH( TRIM(last_name))
FROM employee_table
ORDER BY last_name;

Result: 9 rows returned
```

Last name	Characters(Last name)	Characters(Trim(BOTH FROM Last name))
Clooney	20	7
Ford	20	4
Gere	20	4
Mcfly	20	5
Roberts	20	7
Strickland	20	10
Student	20	7
Travolta	20	8
Willis	20	6

Figure 9.6

Note: Notice the heading for column 3.

OCTET Function

This function returns the length of *string_expression* in octets when it is converted to the named character set (taking the export width value into consideration). Since our character set is ASCII, the results will match the CHARACTERS count.

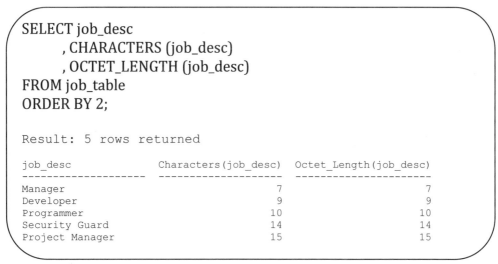

```
SELECT job_desc
     , CHARACTERS (job_desc)
     , OCTET_LENGTH (job_desc)
FROM job_table
ORDER BY 2;


Result: 5 rows returned

job_desc                Characters(job_desc)  Octet_Length(job_desc)
--------------------    --------------------  ----------------------
Manager                                    7                       7
Developer                                  9                       9
Programmer                                10                      10
Security Guard                            14                      14
Project Manager                           15                      15
```

Figure 9.7

POSITION

Another useful function is POSITION. It returns the starting position of *string-1* within *string-2.* It is frequently combined with the SUBSTRING or SUBSTR function. If *string-2* is numeric, it will be converted to CHARACTER.

The following is a simple example of the POSITION function.

```
SELECT  job_desc
      , POSITION ('Ma' IN job_desc)
FROM   job_table
ORDER BY 1;

Result: 5 rows returned

job_desc                 Position('Ma' in job_desc)
--------------------     --------------------------
Developer                                         0
Manager                                           1
Programmer                                        0
Project Manager                                   9
Security Guard                                    0
```

Figure 9.8

INDEX

As shown in the Figure 9.9, the INDEX function is a Teradata extension. It functions just like POSITION, and returns the starting position of string-2 within string-1. Use POSITION for ANSI compatibility.

The following query is the same as the previous query (Figure 9.8) but uses the INDEX function.

```
SELECT  job_desc
      , INDEX(job_desc, 'ma')
FROM   job_table
ORDER BY 1;

Result: 5 rows returned

job_desc                 Index(job_desc,'ma')
--------------------     --------------------
Developer                                   0
Manager                                     1
Programmer                                  0
Project Manager                             9
Security Guard                              0
```

Figure 9.9

SUBSTRING and SUBSTR

The SUBSTRING and SUBSTR function identically and extract a substring from a string starting at a given character position for a given number of characters. SUBSTRING is the ANSI version of the Teradata SUBSTR. If the string is numeric it is converted to CHARACTER.

ANSI syntax: SUBSTRING (string-1 FROM p-1 [FOR c-1])

Teradata syntax: SUBSTR (string-1, p-1 [,c-1])

Where p-1 is the starting position and c-1 is the length of the substring to be extracted. If c-1 is omitted, the default is end-of-string.

The following example uses both functions to extract the first 5 characters from each course name.

```
SELECT course_name
      , SUBSTRING (course_name FROM 1 FOR 5) AS "Substring"
      , SUBSTR (course_name, 1, 5) AS "Substr"
FROM   course_table
ORDER BY 1;

Result: 6 rows returned

Course_name                        Substring   Substr
--------------------------------   ---------   ------
Advanced SQL                       Advan       Advan
Database Administration            Datab       Datab
Introduction to SQL                Intro       Intro
Physical Database Tuning           Physi       Physi
TD12 SQL Features                  TD12        TD12
Teradata Basics                    Terad       Terad
```

Figure 9.10

SUBSTRING and POSITION

If the starting position for an extract varies from row to row, based upon some defined value, use POSITION to locate the value and extract from that point.

The next example extracts all words of the course name after the first word.

```
SELECT course_name
      , SUBSTRING(course_name FROM
          POSITION(' ' IN course_name)) AS "SUBSTRING"
FROM course_table
ORDER BY 1 ;

Result: 6 rows returned

Course_name                          SUBSTRING
-------------------------------      -------------------
Advanced SQL                         SQL
Database Administration              Administration
Introduction to SQL                  to SQL
Physical Database Tuning             Database Tuning
TD12 SQL Features                    SQL Features
Teradata Basics                      Basics
```

Figure 9.11

Because POSITION returns the value of the first space character in this example, the space is included in the result. To eliminate this space, do the following.

```
SELECT course_name
     , SUBSTRING(course_name FROM
        POSITION(' ' IN course_name) + 1) AS "SUBSTRING"
FROM course_table
ORDER BY 1 ;

Result: 6 rows returned

Course_name                      SUBSTRING
------------------------------   -----------------
Advanced SQL                     SQL
Database Administration          Administration
Introduction to SQL              to SQL
Physical Database Tuning         Database Tuning
TD12 SQL Features                SQL Features
Teradata Basics                  Basics
```

Figure 9.12

Practice Questions

1. Which of the following are Teradata extensions?
   a. INDEX
   b. UPPER
   c. SUBSTR
   d. CHARACTERS
   e. BYTES
   f. SELECT DEFAULT
   g. SELECT FORMAT
   h. All of the above

2. TRIM(col1) and TRIM(BOTH FROM col1) are equivalent.
   a. TRUE
   b. FALSE

3. Which of the following will remove leading zeroes from a numeric column?
   a. TRIM(LEADING 0 FROM col1)
   b. TRIM(LEADING '0' FROM col1)

4. Choose the correct result from the following query.
   SELECT trim(' a ') || trim(leading from ' b ') || trim(trailing from ' c ') || 'd';
   a. a bcd
   b. abcd
   c. ab c d
   d. ab   cd

5. Choose the correct result from the following query.
   SELECT SUBSTRING('abcdef' FROM -2 FOR 6);
   - a. a
   - b. ab
   - c. abc
   - d. abcd
   - e. abcde
   - f. abcdef

6. Choose the correct result from the following query.
   SELECT POSITION('de' IN 'abcdefg');
   - a. 3
   - b. 4
   - c. 5

Chapter Notes

Utilize this space for notes, key points to remember, diagrams, areas of further study, etc.

_____

_____

_____

_____

_____

_____

_____

_____

_____

_____

_____

_____

_____

Chapter 10: OLAP Functions

Certification Objectives

- ✓ Describe the functionality of Ordered/On-Line Analytic Functions (OLAP).
- ✓ Given an answer set, identify the Window Aggregate function.
- ✓ Describe the functionality of RANK.
- ✓ Identify characteristics of a query that indicates optimization opportunities.
- ✓ Given a scenario, identify the number of rows returned by SAMPLE.
- ✓ Identify the functionality of TOP N.
- ✓ Identify the processing differences between TOP N and SAMPLE.

Before You Begin

You should be familiar with the following terms and concepts.

Terms	Key Concepts
Sum / Over	Understand the SQL syntax for cumulative summation of data
Rank	How to apply and reset capabilities
Row_Number	Utilization of this function to number resulting rows
Sample / Top	How do these functions work and the differences

Teradata On-Line Analytical Processing Functions

The OLAP and aggregate functions are close cousins, but are very different in their use. Like traditional aggregates, OLAP functions operate on groups of rows and permit qualification and filtering of the group result. Unlike aggregates that return a single aggregated value, OLAP functions also return the individual row detail.

The following chart contains the Teradata OLAP aggregates and their functions. These are supported only for backward compatibility.

Teradata Extensions

DEPRECATED TERADATA EXTENSIONS	DESCRIPTION	EQUIVALENT ANSI SQL-2003 WINDOW FUNCTIONS
CSUM	Cumulative sum of a referenced value, for a range or dimension.	SUM
MAVG	Computation of a moving average of a referenced value based on a specified window.	AVG
MDIFF	Computation of a moving difference between two referenced data values based on a specified window.	Composable from SUM
MLINREG	Computation of a moving linear regression between two referenced data values based on a specified window.	Composable from SUM and COUNT

MSUM	Computation of a moving sum of a referenced value based on a specified window.	SUM
RANK	Ranking based on high order or low order of a referenced data value based on a specified value.	RANK

Figure 10.1

Though there are more OLAP functions, the following chart shows some of the more frequently used ANSI OLAP commands and their functions:

ANSI OLAP Functions

Command	Functionality
SUM/OVER	Cumulative sum of a referenced value, for a range or dimension.
SUM / OVER (Moving Sum)	Computation of a moving sum of a referenced value, based on a specified window.
RANK / OVER	Ranking based on high order or low order of a referenced data value, based on a specified value.
RANK / OVER (QUANTILE)	Categorize a referenced data value, based on a number of partitions.
ROW_NUMBER / OVER	Assigns a unique number to each row to which it is applied, either each row in the partition or each row returned by the query. In the ordered sequence of rows specified in the order by clause, the rows begin with the number one.

Figure 10.2

In the following chart, the OVER Windows definitions are presented.

OVER (. . .) WINDOW DEFINITIONS

PARTITION BY col1 [, ... , coln]	Defines the "GROUP" or "Window" of rows over which the aggregate function operates. If there is no PARTITION BY clause, then the entire result set, delivered by the FROM clause, constitutes a single group or partition.	
ORDER BY value_expression [ASC	DESC]	The ordering of rows within the Group, not the final result.	
ROWS	The starting point for the aggregation group within the partition. The aggregation group end is the current row. The aggregation group of a row R is a set of rows, defined relative to R in the ordering of the rows within the partition. If there is no ROWS or ROWS BETWEEN clause, the default aggregation group is ROWS BETWEEN UNBOUNDED PRECEDING AND UNBOUNDED FOLLOWING.	
	UNBOUNDED PRECEDING	Include all group rows preceding the current row.
	Value PRECEDING	Include the specified number of rows before the current row.
	CURRENT ROW	Report only on the current row.

ROWS BETWEEN	The aggregation group start and end, which defines a set of rows relative to the current row in the ordering of the rows within the partition. The row specified by the group start must precede the row specified by the group end. If there is no ROWS or ROWS BETWEEN clause, the default aggregation group is ROWS BETWEEN UNBOUNDED PRECEDING AND UNBOUNDED FOLLOWING.	
	UNBOUNDED PRECEDING AND	UNBOUNDED FOLLOWING
		value PRECEDING
		CURRENT ROW
		value FOLLOWING
	value PRECEDING AND	UNBOUNDED FOLLOWING
		value PRECEDING
		CURRENT ROW
		value FOLLOWING
	CURRENT ROW AND	UNBOUNDED FOLLOWING
		CURRENT ROW
		value FOLLOWING
	value FOLLOWING AND	UNBOUNDED FOLLOWING
		value FOLLOWING

Figure 10.3

General Syntax:

aggregate_function OVER([PARTITION BY] [ORDER BY] [ROWS | ROWS BETWEEN])

The best way to understand the OLAP functions is by studying the following examples.

Cumulative SUM - SUM / OVER

The next example demonstrates the ANSI SUM / OVER. It produces the same result as the Teradata CSUM function.

```
SELECT  Product_ID
        ,Sale_Date
        ,Daily_Sales
        ,SUM(Daily_Sales)
          OVER ( ORDER BY Sale_Date
          ROWS UNBOUNDED PRECEDING) AS  Like_CSum
FROM  Sales_table
WHERE Product_ID BETWEEN 1000 and 2000 ;

Result: 14 rows returned

Product_ID  Sale_Date  Daily_Sales    Like_CSum
----------  ---------  -----------    ----------
      1000   07/09/28     45850.40     45850.40
      2000   07/09/28     42787.88     88638.28
      1000   07/09/29     64500.22    153138.50
      2000   07/09/29     46090.00    199228.50
      2000   07/09/30     44850.03    244078.53
      1000   07/09/30     36000.07    280078.60
      2000   07/10/01     58850.29    338928.89
      1000   07/10/01     45700.43    384629.32
      2000   07/10/02     35599.93    420229.25
      1000   07/10/02     33700.50    453929.75
      2000   07/10/03     41900.18    495829.93
      1000   07/10/03     66200.00    562029.93
      2000   07/10/04     32878.50    594908.43
      1000   07/10/04     54575.10    649483.53
```

Figure 10.4

Note: In this example, all rows participate as a single group.

SUM Using SUM / OVER and PARTITION BY

The ANSI method does not use GROUP BY. Instead, it uses the OVER to designate that a partition or group can be established using the PARTITION BY indicator.

```
SELECT Product_ID
      ,Sale_Date
      ,Daily_Sales
      ,SUM(Daily_Sales)
        OVER ( PARTITION BY Sale_Date
         ORDER BY Sale_Date  ROWS UNBOUNDED PRECEDING)
        (format '$$$$,$$$.99')  AS  Like_CSum
FROM  Sales_table
WHERE Sale_Date between 1071001 and 1071003 ;

Result: 9 rows returned

Product_ID  Sale_Date  Daily_Sales    Like_CSum
----------- ---------- -----------   -----------
      2000   07/10/01     58850.29   $58,850.29
      3000   07/10/01     27000.00   $85,850.29
      1000   07/10/01     45700.43   $131,550.72
      1000   07/10/02     33700.50   $33,700.50
      2000   07/10/02     35599.93   $69,300.43
      3000   07/10/02     18767.94   $88,068.37
      1000   07/10/03     66200.00   $66,200.00
      2000   07/10/03     41900.18   $108,100.18
      3000   07/10/03     21553.79   $129,653.97
```

Figure 10.5

Ranking Data using the ANSI RANK / OVER

The output of the RANK / OVER function is the highest or the lowest data values in the column, depending on the sort requested. A query can return a specified number of the "best" rows (highest values) or the "worst" rows (lowest values). These capabilities and output options will be demonstrated below.

Here is the syntax for RANK / OVER:

RANK() OVER ([PARTITION BY <column-name> [...,<column-number>]] ORDER BY <column-list> [DESC | ASC])

The next SELECT operates over all of the rows in the Sales table, ranking daily sales in best-to-worst (DESC) order.

```
SELECT        Product_ID
              ,Sale_Date
              ,Daily_Sales
              ,RANK() OVER (ORDER BY daily_sales DESC)  AS
"RANK"
FROM  Sales_table ;


Result: 21 rows returned

Product_ID  Sale_Date  Daily_Sales          RANK
----------- ---------  -----------  -----------
      1000  07/10/03     66200.00            1
      1000  07/09/29     64500.22            2
      3000  07/09/28     60903.77            3
      2000  07/10/01     58850.29            4
      1000  07/10/04     54575.10            5
      2000  07/09/29     46090.00            6
      1000  07/09/28     45850.40            7
      1000  07/10/01     45700.43            8
      2000  07/09/30     44850.03            9
      2000  07/09/28     42787.88           10
      3000  07/09/30     42338.86           11
      2000  07/10/03     41900.18           12
      1000  07/09/30     36000.07           13
      2000  07/10/02     35599.93           14
      3000  07/09/29     34654.13           15
      1000  07/10/02     33700.50           16
      2000  07/10/04     32878.50           17
      3000  07/10/01     27000.00           18
      3000  07/10/03     21553.79           19
      3000  07/10/02     18767.94           20
      3000  07/10/04     14875.33           21
```

Figure 10.6

To make the report show daily sales in worst-to-best ranking order, change the ORDER BY to ASC (default).

QUALIFY to Find Top Best or Bottom Worse

The above report could have been created without the window functions by simply listing all rows in decreasing sales amount. With a small number of rows, the best and the worst is readily available. However, when there are hundreds or millions of rows, returning all the rows takes far too much time.

The QUALIFY function operates on window group output the same way the HAVING clause does for GROUP BY groups. It's either GROUP BY ... HAVING, or OVER(...) QUALIFY.

The following SELECT is the same as the above, but uses the QUALIFY to limit the output to the best 3 (highest values) rows:

```
SELECT        Product_ID
              ,Sale_Date
              ,Daily_Sales
              ,RANK() OVER (ORDER BY Daily_Sales DESC) AS
"RANK"
FROM  Sales_table
QUALIFY "RANK" < 4 ;

Result: 3 rows returned

Product_ID  Sale_Date  Daily_Sales        RANK
----------- ---------- -----------   -----------
       1000  07/10/03    66200.00             1
       1000  07/09/29    64500.22             2
       3000  07/09/28    60903.77             3
```

Figure 10.7

The next SELECT is the same as the above, with one exception. It uses the ASC to reverse the default sequence of DESC. Now, the worst (lowest) 3 values are returned:

```
SELECT      Product_ID
            ,Sale_Date
            ,Daily_Sales
            ,RANK() OVER (ORDER BY Daily_Sales ASC) AS "RANK"
FROM  Sales_table
QUALIFY "RANK" < 4 ;

Result: 3 rows returned

Product_ID  Sale_Date  Daily_Sales      RANK
----------- ---------- ----------- -----------
      3000   07/10/04     14875.33           1
      3000   07/10/02     18767.94           2
      3000   07/10/03     21553.79           3
```

Figure 10.8

RANK with Reset Capabilities

There is a method available to reset a RANK / OVER function to provide the best or worst rank of a group of rows that contain a common value in another column. Use the PARTITION BY designation to specify a data value that, when it changes, causes the accumulation value to be reset back to zero. Figure 10.9 demonstrates the reset option.

Using RANK/OVER with PARTITION BY

The following SELECT ranks the daily sales for each product using the PARTITION BY and creates an alias for the RANK column to use in the QUALIFY to find the best 2 days:

```
SELECT       Product_ID
             ,Sale_Date
             ,Daily_Sales
             ,RANK()  OVER (PARTITION BY Product_ID
                      ORDER BY Daily_Sales DESC )  AS Ranked
FROM  Sales_table
QUALIFY Ranked <= 2 ;

Result: 6 rows returned

Product_ID  Sale_Date  Daily_Sales        Ranked
----------- ---------- ------------       -----------
       1000   07/10/03    66200.00              1
       1000   07/09/29    64500.22              2
       2000   07/10/01    58850.29              1
       2000   07/09/29    46090.00              2
       3000   07/09/28    60903.77              1
       3000   07/09/30    42338.86              2
```

Figure 10.9

Numbering of the Rows Using ROW_NUMBER / OVER

The following ANSI syntax is used with ROW_NUMBER to provide OLAP functionality. At the same time, it can be used to generate a sequential number.

ROW_NUMBER() OVER ([PARTITION BY <value-column-data>]
                    ORDER BY <column-list>)

The next SELECT uses ROW_NUMBER to produce a report for the dates in September:

```
SELECT      Product_ID
            ,Sale_Date
            ,Daily_Sales   (Format '$$$,$$$.99')
            ,ROW_NUMBER() OVER ( ORDER BY product_id,
                    daily_sales desc) AS "Row Number"
FROM  Sales_table
WHERE EXTRACT(MONTH FROM Sale_Date) = 9 ;

Result: 9 rows returned

Product_ID  Sale_Date  Daily_Sales   Row Number
----------- ---------- ------------  -----------
       1000  07/09/29   $64,500.22             1
       1000  07/09/28   $45,850.40             2
       1000  07/09/30   $36,000.07             3
       2000  07/09/29   $46,090.00             4
       2000  07/09/30   $44,850.03             5
       2000  07/09/28   $42,787.88             6
       3000  07/09/28   $60,903.77             7
       3000  07/09/30   $42,338.86             8
       3000  07/09/29   $34,654.13             9
```

Figure 10.10

The next SELECT uses ROW_NUMBER / OVER to produce a similar report as the previous functions, sorting and breaking on the Product ID:

```
SELECT      Product_ID
            ,Sale_Date
            ,Daily_Sales          (Format '$$$,$$$.99')
            ,ROW_NUMBER() OVER (PARTITION BY product_id
                                  ORDER BY product_id,
daily_sales desc )
                                   AS "Row Number"
FROM   Sales_table
WHERE EXTRACT(MONTH FROM Sale_Date) = 9;

Result: 9 rows returned

 Product_ID  Sale_Date   Daily_Sales   Row Number
 ----------  ---------   -----------   -----------
       1000   07/09/29   $64,500.22             1
       1000   07/09/28   $45,850.40             2
       1000   07/09/30   $36,000.07             3
       2000   07/09/29   $46,090.00             1
       2000   07/09/30   $44,850.03             2
       2000   07/09/28   $42,787.88             3
       3000   07/09/28   $60,903.77             1
       3000   07/09/30   $42,338.86             2
       3000   07/09/29   $34,654.13             3
```

Figure 10.11

SAMPLE and SAMPLEID

The SAMPLE function reduces the number of rows to be considered for further processing by returning one or more samples of rows specified either as a list of fractions of the total number of rows or as a list of numbers of rows from the SELECT query. This is a Teradata extension.

Syntax:

SAMPLE [WITH REPLACEMENT] [RANDOMIZED ALLOCATION]
{ [{*fraction_description* | *count_description* } |
WHEN *condition* THEN {*fraction_description* | *count_description* }
[ELSE {*fraction_description* | *count_description*] } END
}

Syntax element . . .	Specifies . . .
WITH REPLACEMENT	whether sampling is done by returning each sampled row to the table for possible redundant sampling or by withholding sampled rows from resampling. If you specify WITH REPLACEMENT, then it is possible to request more samples than there are rows in the table. Sampling without replacement is the default. You select it implicitly by not specifying WITH REPLACEMENT.

RANDOMIZED ALLOCATION	whether rows are sampled randomly across AMPS (RANDOMIZED ALLOCATION) or proportionate to the number of qualified rows per AMP (proportional allocation). The proportional allocation option does not provide a simple random sample of the entire population. It provides a random sample stratified by AMPs, but it is much faster, especially for very large samples. Proportional is the default. You select it implicitly by not specifying RANDOMIZED ALLOCATION.
fraction_description	any set of unsigned floating point constant numbers in the closed interval (0,1) that specifies the percentage of rows to be sampled for a true search condition. This is a comma-separated list of fractions, the sum of which must not exceed 1. The value set specifies the percentage of the homogeneous subgroup defined by *search_condition* to be sampled for the report. No more than 16 samples can be requested per fraction description.

| count_description | a set of positive integer constants that specifies the number of rows to be sampled for a true search condition.

A warning is returned if there are not enough rows in the result to satisfy the sampling request completely.

No more than 16 samples can be requested per count description. |
|---|---|
| WHEN | to test a set of conditions for truth. |
| condition | an evaluation predicate that defines each homogeneous subgroup in the sample set. |
| THEN | to apply the specified sampling fraction description or count description to the sample. |
| ELSE | to apply the specified sampling fraction description or count description to the sample if none of the WHEN condition predicates evaluates to true. |
| END | the termination of the WHEN ... THEN ... ELSE clause. |

Figure 10.12

In the following query, all of the rows will be included in the sample since the fraction description sums to 100%.

```
SELECT product_id
     , sale_date
     , daily_sales
FROM sales_table
SAMPLE .1, .2, .3, .4
ORDER BY sale_date, product_id;

Result: 20 rows returned

Product_ID   Sale_Date   Daily_Sales
-----------  ----------  -----------
       1000   07/09/28      45850.40
       2000   07/09/28      42787.88
       3000   07/09/28      60903.77
       1000   07/09/29      64500.22
       2000   07/09/29      46090.00
       3000   07/09/29      34654.13
       1000   07/09/30      36000.07
       2000   07/09/30      44850.03
       1000   07/10/01      45700.43
       2000   07/10/01      58850.29
       3000   07/10/01      27000.00
       1000   07/10/02      33700.50
       2000   07/10/02      35599.93
       3000   07/10/02      18767.94
       1000   07/10/03      66200.00
       2000   07/10/03      41900.18
       3000   07/10/03      21553.79
       1000   07/10/04      54575.10
       2000   07/10/04      32878.50
       3000   07/10/04      14875.33
```

Figure 10.13

SAMPLEID, which is a Teradata extension, identifies the sample to which a row belongs in the left-to-right order of the SAMPLE clause specification; from 1 through n (where n is the number of samples requested in the SAMPLE clause).

Since the sales_table contains 21 rows, the first sample of .1 (or 10%) will contain 2 rows, the second sample .2 (or 20%), etc..

The following query shows the SampleId generated values.

```
SELECT product_id
     , sale_date
     , daily_sales
     , SAMPLEID
FROM sales_table
SAMPLE .1, .2, .3, .4
ORDER BY  sale_date, product_id;

Result:   20 rows returned

Product_ID  Sale_Date  Daily_Sales      SampleId
----------  ---------  -----------      --------
      1000   07/09/28     45850.40             3
      2000   07/09/28     42787.88             3
      3000   07/09/28     60903.77             3
      1000   07/09/29     64500.22             3
      2000   07/09/29     46090.00             2
      3000   07/09/29     34654.13             4
      1000   07/09/30     36000.07             1
      2000   07/09/30     44850.03             4
      3000   07/09/30     42338.86             2
      1000   07/10/01     45700.43             2
      2000   07/10/01     58850.29             3
      3000   07/10/01     27000.00             3
      1000   07/10/02     33700.50             4
      3000   07/10/02     18767.94             4
      1000   07/10/03     66200.00             4
      2000   07/10/03     41900.18             4
      3000   07/10/03     21553.79             1
      1000   07/10/04     54575.10             4
      2000   07/10/04     32878.50             2
      3000   07/10/04     14875.33             4
```

Figure 10.14

TOP [n] [WITH TIES]

The TOP n allows the user to specify how many rows are to be returned from the query result set. The value of n may be specified as either a positive integer or a positive decimal number. If PERCENT is not specified, the decimal number may not contain a decimal point. If *n* is greater than the actual number of rows, all rows are returned without error.

```
SELECT TOP 3
      student_id
    , last_name
    , class_code
FROM student_table;

Result: 3 rows returned

Student_ID  Last_name               Class_code
----------- ----------------------  ----------
    280023  Rieter                     JR
    423400  Lamp                       FR
    322133  Bond                       JR
```

Figure 10.15

The WITH TIES option only applies to a SELECT statement that also specifies an ORDER BY clause. In addition to returning the specified number or percentage of rows in the ordered set produced by the ORDER BY clause, the query should return any rows where the sort value is the same as the sort value in the last row that satisfies the specified number or percentage of rows. The next query demonstrates this.

```
SELECT TOP 3 WITH TIES
        student_id
      , last_name
      , class_code
FROM student_table
ORDER BY class_code ;

Student_ID  Last_name              Class_code
----------  --------------------   ----------
    260000  Johnson                ?
    423400  Lamp                   FR
    234121  Garrett                FR
    125634  Kojack                 FR
```

Figure 10.16

Note: Though we requested only three rows, four were returned. In best-case scenarios, the TOP option provides better performance over SAMPLE. In worst-case scenarios, the TOP option provides equivalent performance.

Practice Questions

1. The WITH TIES is only meaningful if:
   a. The TOP n specifies a percentage instead of a row count.
   b. The TOP n specifies a row count instead of a percentage.
   c. The query does not contain an ORDER BY.
   d. None of the above.

2. SAMPLE and SAMPLEID are ANSI functions.
   a. TRUE
   b. FALSE

3. ROW_NUMBER OVER
   a. Ignores window partition boundaries.
   b. Resets back to 1 for each window partition.

4. RANK OVER and PARTITION BY are mutually exclusive.
   a. TRUE
   b. FALSE

5. HAVING does for GROUP BY groups what _____ does for window groups.
   a. RANK
   b. PARTITION
   c. ORDER BY
   d. QUALIFY
   e. SAMPLE

6. The RANK function is:
    a. A Teradata extension.
    b. An ANSI function.

7. SAMPLE and TOPn
    a. Can never return the same row more than once.
    b. Both can return the same row more than once.
    c. Only TOP n can return the same row more than once.
    d. Only SAMPLE can return the same row more than once.

Chapter Notes

Utilize this space for notes, key points to remember, diagrams, areas of further study, etc.

_____

_____

_____

_____

_____

_____

_____

_____

_____

_____

_____

_____

_____

Chapter 11: Set Operators

Certification Objectives

- ✓ Identify the types set operators.
- ✓ Given a scenario, identify the number of rows returned using UNION and UNION ALL.

Before You Begin

You should be familiar with the following terms and concepts.

Terms	Key Concepts
Set Operators	Considerations and restrictions
UNION / INTERSECT	Knowledge on how to apply
EXCEPT / MINUS	How do these functions eliminate rows
Multiple Operators	Understand the order of precedence

The set operator(s) let you combine the results from two or more SELECT statements to construct more complex queries. Teradata supports three classes of set operations:

UNION [DISTINCT] and UNION ALL
INTERSECT [DISTINCT] and INTERSECT ALL
EXCEPT [DISTINCT] or MINUS [DISTINCT] and EXCEPT ALL, MINUS ALL

The ALL option (which allows duplicate rows to be returned), and the MINUS operator, are Teradata extensions.

Set Operations - Restrictions

SQL statements that contain set operators are called compound queries. In order for a compound query to work successfully, the following conditions must exist:

- The result sets of both queries must have the same number of columns.
- The corresponding columns in the queries must have the same data type or must be implicitly convertible to the same data type.
- If the names of the columns match, SQL uses that column name in the answer set.
- If the column names are different, SQL uses the names from the first query in the set operation. Use an AS clause in the first query if you want to rename a column.
- You can specify an optional ORDER BY clause only in the final query in the set statement. SQL applies the sort to the final combined result.
- You can specify GROUP BY and HAVING only in individual queries. You cannot use them to affect the result.
- WITH and WITH ... BY cannot be used.

UNION

The UNION operation combines the results of two subqueries into a single result that consists of all of the rows from both queries. A UNION removes duplicate rows from the result set. It is the equivalent of a FULL OUTER JOIN.

The following query shows the UNION operator.

```
SELECT dept_no FROM department_table
UNION
SELECT dept_no FROM employee_table
ORDER BY 1 ;

Result: 7 rows returned

Dept_No
-------
      ?
     10
    100
    200
    300
    400
    500
```

Figure 11.1

Note: Set operator results evaluate to the data type of the columns defined in the first SELECT statement in the operation. When a column in the first SELECT is defined as an explicit NULL, the data type of the result is not intuitive.

UNION ALL

A UNION ALL expression allows for all the duplicates to be displayed. Remember that the ALL option is a Teradata extension. The next example demonstrates this.

```
SELECT dept_no FROM department_table
UNION ALL
SELECT dept_no FROM employee_table
ORDER BY 1 ;

Result: 14 rows returned

Dept_No
-------
      ?
     10
    100
    100
    200
    200
    200
    300
    300
    400
    400
    400
    400
    500
```

Figure 11.2

Teradata 12 Certification Study Guide

The following query answers the questions, "Who is manager 1121334, and who works for him?".

```
SELECT  first_name
        , last_name
        , 'employee' AS Employee_Type
FROM    employee_table
WHERE mgr_employee_no = 1121334
UNION
SELECT first_name
        , last_name
        , 'manager'
FROM    employee_table
WHERE employee_no = 1121334
ORDER BY 3 DESC , 2 ;


Result: 4 rows returned

First_name      Last_name               Employee_Type
-----------     --------------------    -------------
Stan            Strickland              manager
Richard         Gere                    employee
Julia           Roberts                 employee
John            Travolta                employee
```

Figure 11.3

Remember that the first query determines the column names for the output.

INTERSECT

The INTERSECT operator combines the results of two queries into a single result set that consists of only the common rows they share. It is the equivalent of an INNER JOIN.

List all managers having subordinate employees.

```
SELECT mgr_employee_no FROM employee_table
INTERSECT
SELECT mgr_no FROM department_table
ORDER BY 1 ;

Result: 4 rows returned

Mgr_Employee_No
---------------
        1000234
        1121334
        1256349
        1333454
```

Figure 11.4

EXCEPT/MINUS

The EXCEPT/MINUS operation returns only the rows that are unique to the first query, removing any rows that it has in common with the second query. It is the equivalent of doing a LEFT OUTER JOIN – INNER JOIN. The MINUS operator is a Teradata extension.

The next query answers the request, "find the departments that do not have any employees".

```
SELECT  Dept_no AS Department_Number
FROM    Department_Table
EXCEPT
SELECT Dept_no
FROM   Employee_Table ;


or


SELECT  Dept_no AS Department_Number
FROM    Department_Table
MINUS
SELECT Dept_no
FROM   Employee_Table ;

Result: 1 row returned

Department_Number
-----------------
              500
```

Figure 11.5

Multiple Set Operators and Precedence Order

If multiple operators appear in the same query, SQL executes them from left to right. The INTERSECT function takes higher precedence and will be done first before all other Operators, unless parentheses specify a different order. For example, consider the following example:

SELECT statement_1
UNION
SELECT statement_2
EXCEPT
SELECT statement_3
INTERSECT
SELECT statement_4;

The operations are performed in the following order:

1. Intersect the results of statement_3 and statement_4.
2. Union the results of statement_1 and statement_2.
3. Subtract the intersected rows from the union.

As stated earlier in this chapter, the corresponding columns in the queries must have the same data type or must be implicitly convertible to the same data type. The following query satisfies this requirement, but produces results that are meaningless. It combines employee numbers and job numbers in the same column.

```
SELECT emp_no FROM emp_job_table
WHERE job_no=20010
INTERSECT
SELECT employee_no FROM employee_table
UNION
SELECT job_no FROM job_table
WHERE job_desc LIKE 'Prog%' ;

Result: 4 rows returned

     emp_no
-----------
      20010
    1121334
    1324657
    2341218
```

Figure 11.6

Though the corresponding columns in the queries have the same data type, the data values come from different domains.

Practice Questions

1. Unless parenthesis specify a different order, the normal order of evaluation of the Set operators is:
   a. Left to right
   b. UNION first, then left to right
   c. EXCEPT first, then left to right
   d. INTERSECT first, then left to right

2. Which set operator is the equivalent of an inner join?
   a. INTERSECT
   b. EXCEPT
   c. UNION

3. The EXCEPT operator is a Teradata extension.
   a. TRUE
   b. FALSE

4. The ALL extension only applies to the UNION operator.
   a. TRUE
   b. FALSE

5. In combining queries using set operators, an ORDER BY clause:
   a. May appear in any query.
   b. Can only appear in the first query.
   c. Can only appear in the last query.

6. The column names of the last query are used for output.
   a. TRUE
   b. FALSE

Chapter Notes

Utilize this space for notes, key points to remember, diagrams, areas of further study, etc.

_____

_____

_____

_____

_____

_____

_____

_____

_____

_____

_____

_____

_____

_____

_____

Teradata 12 Certification Study Guide

Chapter 12: Data Manipulation

Certification Objectives

- ✓ Identify a correctly written insert statement.
- ✓ Identify a correctly written update statement.
- ✓ Identify a correctly written delete statement.
- ✓ Identify a correctly written select statement.
- ✓ Identify the factors that influence the decision to use ANSI MERGE INTO and UPDATE (upsert processing).

Before You Begin

You should be familiar with the following terms and concepts.

Terms	Key Concepts
Data Maintenance	Consideration and safeguards
DML	INSERT, UPDATE, UPSERT, and DELETE commands
Merge-Into	Understanding how this function works, and the benefits

The following Data Manipulation Language (DML) commands enable you to remove, add, and modify data:

- DELETE - Removes rows from a table
- INSERT- Adds a new row to a table
- INSERT/SELECT adds rows to a table from another table
- UPDATE- Replaces values of columns in a table
- UPSERT – Updates a row or inserts a new one

DELETE

The DELETE command is used to remove rows from a table that satisfy a condition based on a WHERE clause. This example illustrates a DELETE statement that has a join to another table. This is a Teradata extension to an ANSI standard delete.

```
DELETE FROM order_table_new
WHERE          customer_table.customer_number =
order_table_new.customer_number
AND    order_table_new.order_date='07-01-2009';
```

Figure 12.1

To remove all rows from a table, do the following:

```
DELETE FROM order_table_new;
or
DELETE FROM order_table_new ALL;
```

Figure 12.2

A DELETE FROM <tablename> ALL is very efficient. Since table and index rows of every table are contained within their own data blocks, Teradata simply moves those blocks to the Free Space list. The ALL is the default and is used when a WHERE condition is not specified. Lastly, the ALL option is a non-ANSI Teradata extension.

Tip: Do not use DROP TABLE just to empty a table. In addition to deleting all data and index rows, DROP TABLE also removes the table's definition which can cause a high degree of dictionary contention.

INSERT

Next statement is the INSERT which is used to add rows into a table. This example inserts a single row to the employee table with the fields in the CREATE TABLE column order:

INSERT INTO employee_table
VALUES (3121445, , null, 'Redding', 'Lisa', 53560.00);

Figure 12.3

Notice the two ways of specifying missing data values: skipping the column by just entering a comma, and using the keyword NULL.

To specify a different order of data input, list the columns in the order of the data values:

INSERT INTO employee_table (first_name, last_name,
                    employee_no, salary)
VALUES ('Lisa', 'Redding', 3121445, 53560.00);

Figure 12.4

Note: Since the column names for dept_no and mgr_employee_no do not appear in the column list, the system will insert nulls. If a column has been declared NOT NULL, then a value for that column must be supplied. You can also specify a logging option with an INSERT which will do error handling.

INSERT/SELECT

This command is used to copy rows, or a subset of rows, from one table to another. The following is a simple INSERT/SELECT example:

```
INSERT INTO emp_new
SELECT * FROM employee_table ;
```

Figure 12.5

Assumes:
- emp_new and employee_table have the same definitions
- a complete replica of employee_table is required

Two different optimizations can occur:
1. If the PI of the source AND destination tables are identical, an AMP local operation is used.
2. If the target table is empty,
   a.) Transient Journaling is reduced
   b.) 64K block transfers are used

If both conditions are satisfied, both optimizations are used. Below is a more complex example:

```
CREATE TABLE sales_analysis
(sales_count SMALLINT, yr_mo INTEGER, sales_total DECIMAL (9,2))
PRIMARY INDEX (sales_count);

INSERT INTO sales_analysis
SELECT COUNT(*), sale_date/100, SUM(daily_sales)
FROM sales_table
GROUP BY 2 ;

SELECT * FROM sales_analysis;

Result: 2 rows returned

sales_count          yr_mo   sales_total
-----------      -----------  -----------
          9           10709    417975.36
         12           10710    451601.99
```

Figure 12.6

UPSERT

Teradata has another extension to the Update command called an UPSERT. The query checks to see if the row exists in the table and updates it if found. If nothing is found a new row is inserted.

There are several restrictions that need to be considered when deciding to use an UPSERT, which are outlined below:

1. The update and the insert portions must reference the same row of the same table using the rows PI value to do the operation. The PI can't be an Identity column. If these rules are not followed, an error is returned.

2. For tables with PPI, there are additional restrictions. Both statements have to specify the same partition. The update can't modify partitioning columns and all the partitioning columns must be in the WHERE clause.

The example below shows a simple UPSERT statement.

```
UPDATE job_table
SET job_desc = 'Gopher'
WHERE job_no = 12345  /* Non-existent job number */
ELSE
INSERT INTO job_table
VALUES (12345, 'Gopher');
```

Figure 12.7

MERGE

The MERGE-INTO command merges a source row set into a target table based on whether any target rows satisfy a specified matching condition with the source row. MERGE replicates the UPSERT functionality, but over more than one row (i.e. Block Level). It also has fewer restrictions, making it more flexible then the UPSERT.

1. The update and insert portions of the query do not need to reference the same row of the same table. In addition, they both must reference the row's PI value to do their operations. The PI can be an Identity Column

2. For PPI tables, the insert can specify a different partition then the update. The update can modify any partitioning columns but not all the partitioning columns need be in the WHERE clause.

The general MERGE commands are as follows:

MERGE [INTO] *target-table-name*	In the ANSI SQL:2003 definition, this statement is named MERGE INTO, while in the Teradata definition, INTO is an unnecessary noise keyword.
USING	VALUES (*v1* [, ...]) AS *source-table-name (col1* [, ...]) *subquery* AS *source-table-name (col1* [, ...]) *source-table-name* [(COL1 [, ...])]
ON *match-condition*	*match-condition* must specify an equality constraint on the primary index of *target-table* to ensure that the candidate target row set can be hash-accessed on a single AMP. The specified primary index value must match the primary index value implied by the column values specified in the WHEN NOT MATCHED clause.

	WHEN MATCHED THEN UPDATE SET *update-column = update expression* [, ...]
	WHEN NOT MATCHED THEN INSERT [(*col1* [, ...])] VALUES (*val1* [, ...])
[LOGGING]	If logging is not specified, the system does no error handling. If an error occurs, an ANSI request rolls back, and a Teradata transaction aborts and rolls back.

Figure 12.8

LOGGING OPTIONS	
LOGGING [ALL] ERRORS	Log all data errors, reference index errors, and USI errors. If you do not specify a limit, the system defaults to a 10 error limit.
LOGGING ERRORS WITH NO LIMIT	There is no limit to the number of errors that can be logged in the error table associated with the target data table for this MERGE operation, other than the system-determined limit of 16,000,000 errors.
LOGGING ERRORS WITH LIMIT OF *error-limit*	The value you specify for *error_limit* can be anything in the range of 1 to 16,000,000, inclusive. If this limit is exceeded, the system aborts the transaction in Teradata session mode or the request in ANSI session mode, and rolls back all changes made to the target table, but does not roll back the logged error table rows.

Figure 12.9

Below is an MERGE INTO example:

```
MERGE INTO sales_table
USING sales_stage
ON sales_table.product_id = sales_stage.product_id
AND sales_table.sale_date = sales_stage.sale_date
WHEN MATCHED THEN UPDATE SET daily_sales =
sales_stage.daily_sales
WHEN NOT MATCHED THEN INSERT VALUES
(sales_stage.product_id, sales_stage.sale_date, sales_stage.daily_sales)
LOGGING ERRORS WITH LIMIT OF 100;
```

Figure 12.10

ERROR TABLE

The syntax to create an error table is:

CREATE ERROR TABLE *error-table-name* FOR *target-table-name*;

A syntax example is:

```
CREATE ERROR TABLE merge_errors FOR sales_table;

SHOW TABLE merge_errors;
```

Figure 12.11

Practice Questions

1. DELETE FROM t1; and DELETE FROM t1 ALL; are equivalent.
   a. TRUE
   b. FALSE

2. Which is the most efficient way of emptying a table?
   a. DELETE FROM t1 ALL;
   b. DROP TABLE t1;

3. Which command operates over more than one row at a time?
   a. UPSERT
   b. MERGE

4. The correct syntax to create a merge error table is:
   a. CREATE TABLE err_1(c1 INT, c2 CHAR(32000))
      PRIMARY INDEX c1;
   b. CREATE TABLE err_1 FOR target_table;
   c. CREATE ERROR TABLE err1 FOR target_table;

5. Both UPSERT and MERGE can reference PI Identity columns.
   a. TRUE
   b. FALSE

6. Which of the following statements are true?
   a. UPSERT and MERGE must reference the same PPI partition.
   b. UPSERT and MERGE can reference different PPI partitions.
   c. UPSERT can reference different PPI partitions. Merge cannot.
   d. UPSERT must reference the same PPI partition.
   e. MERGE can reference different PPI partitions.

Chapter Notes

Utilize this space for notes, key points to remember, diagrams, areas of further study, etc.

_____

_____

_____

_____

_____

_____

_____

_____

_____

_____

_____

_____

_____

_____

_____

Chapter 13: Data Interrogation

Certification Objectives

- ✓ Given a scenario, identify the result of the CASE expression.
- ✓ Given a scenario, identify the use of special variations of the CASE expression.
- ✓ Given a scenario, identify the use of specialized functions of the CASE expression.

Before You Begin

You should be familiar with the following terms and concepts.

Terms	Key Concepts
CASE	How to apply and understand the options (i.e. Horizontal, Nested, etc.)
COALESCE	Knowledge on how to apply

Data Interrogation is the ability to test column data. It brings conditional logic into the Project list portion of a query. The following functions specify alternate values for a conditional expression or expressions based on equality comparisons and conditions that evaluate to TRUE.

- CASE
- Special variations of the CASE expression:
  - o NULLIF
  - o COALESCE
- Two Teradata extensions
  - o NULLIFZERO
  - o ZEROIFNULL

CASE

- There are two forms of the CASE expression:
    - A valued CASE expression
    - A searched CASE expression
- CASE allows for conditional processing of returned rows.
- CASE returns a single result for each row processed.
- Each row is evaluated against each WHEN clause.
- First match returns a result for that row.
- If no match, the ELSE result is produced for that row.
- CASE is ANSI SQL-2003-compliant.
- WHEN clauses are processed sequentially.
- If no ELSE clause is defined, then the result defaults to NULL.
- The data type of value_expression must be comparable with the data types of all of the value_expression values.
- You can use a scalar subquery in the WHEN clause, THEN clause, and ELSE clause of a CASE expression. If you use a non-scalar subquery (a subquery that returns more than one row), a runtime error is returned.
- If you compare NULL to any value or to NULL, it is always FALSE. If you are testing for a NULL, it is recommended that you use a searched CASE expression with a IS NULL or IS NOT NULL option in the WHEN condition.

Valued CASE Format

```
CASE value-expr WHEN expr1 THEN result1
            WHEN expr2 THEN result2
        ELSE result
        END
```

Teradata 12 Certification Study Guide

The following is an example of a valued case.

```
SELECT   course_name
         ,CASE  credits
               WHEN 1  THEN '1 Credit'
               WHEN 2  THEN '2 Credits'
               WHEN 3  THEN '3 Credits'
               ELSE 'More than 3 Credits'
         END "Number of Credits"
FROM   course_table
ORDER BY credits, 1;


Result: 6 rows returned

Course_name                             Number of Credits
-------------------------------         -------------------
TD12 SQL Features                       2 Credits
Advanced SQL                            3 Credits
Introduction to SQL                     3 Credits
Teradata Basics                         3 Credits
Database Administration                 More than 3 Credits
Physical Database Tuning                More than 3 Credits
```

Figure 13.1

Searched CASE Format

```
CASE  WHEN  condition1 THEN value-expr1
      WHEN  condition2 THEN value-expr2
      ELSE value-expr
      END
```

The following example gives the same result, but is coded as a searched case.

```
SELECT   course_name
         ,CASE
              WHEN credits=1  THEN '1 Credit'
              WHEN credits=2  THEN '2 Credits'
              WHEN credits=3  THEN '3 Credits'
            ELSE 'More than 3 Credits'
          END "Number of Credits"
FROM   course_table
ORDER BY credits, 1;


Result 6 rows returned

Course_name                        Number of Credits
-------------------------------    -------------------
TD12 SQL Features                  2 Credits
Advanced SQL                       3 Credits
Introduction to SQL                3 Credits
Teradata Basics                    3 Credits
Database Administration            More than 3 Credits
Physical Database Tuning           More than 3 Credits
```

Figure 13.2

The WHEN search condition expression has the following rules:

- Can take the form of any comparison operator, such as LIKE, =, or <>.
- Can be a quantified predicate, such as ALL or ANY.
- Can contain a scalar subquery.
- Can contain joins of two tables.
- Cannot contain SELECT statements.

- BLOB's can only be utilized in search_condition, scalar_expression, or scalar_expression when it is cast to BYTE or VARBYTE.
- CLOB's can only be utilized in search_condition, scalar_expression, or scalar_expression when it is cast to CHAR or VARCHAR.

Horizontal CASE Reporting

Typically, SQL row result sets are vertical. CASE allows for horizontal reporting, which displays the row result sets on one line instead of multiple row results.

```
SELECT  AVG(CASE class_code  WHEN 'FR' THEN grade_pt
            ELSE NULL  END) AS Freshman_GPA
       ,AVG(CASE class_code  WHEN 'SO' THEN grade_pt
            ELSE NULL  END) AS Sophomore_GPA
       ,AVG(CASE class_code  WHEN 'JR' THEN grade_pt
            ELSE NULL  END) AS Junior_GPA
       ,AVG(CASE class_code  WHEN 'SR' THEN grade_pt
            ELSE NULL  END) AS Senior_GPA
FROM student_table
WHERE class_code IS NOT NULL;

Result: 1 row returned

Freshman_GPA  Sophomore_GPA   Junior_GPA   Senior_GPA
------------  -------------   ----------   ----------
        2.29           2.90         2.92         3.18
```

Figure 13.3

Nested CASE Expressions

The CASE statement can be nested to check data in a second column from a second CASE statement before determining what value to return.

The following is an example of nested case statements.

```
SELECT last_name
  ,CASE class_code  WHEN 'JR'  THEN 'Junior ' ||
      (CASE WHEN grade_pt < 2  THEN 'Failing'
      WHEN grade_pt < 3.5  THEN 'Passing'  ELSE 'Exceeding'  END)
  ELSE  'Senior ' || (CASE WHEN grade_pt < 2  THEN 'Failing'
      WHEN grade_pt < 3.5  THEN 'Passing'  ELSE 'Exceeding'  END)
      END  AS  Current_Status
FROM student_table
WHERE class_code IN ('JR', 'SR')
ORDER BY class_code, last_name;


Result: 4 rows returned

Last_name                Current_Status
-------------------      ----------------
Bond                     Junior Exceeding
Rieter                   Junior Failing
Craig                    Senior Passing
Phillips                 Senior Passing
```

Figure 13.4

COALESCE

COALESCE returns NULL if all of its arguments evaluate to null. Otherwise, it returns the value of the first non-null argument in the *expression* list.

COALESCE is ANSI SQL-2003-compliant and each COALESCE function must have at least two operands.

Syntax:

COALESCE (expression_1, expression_2 [, expression_n])

COALESCE is a shorthand expression for the following full CASE expression:

CASE
WHEN *expression_1* IS NOT NULL
THEN *expression_1*
...
WHEN *expression_n* IS NOT NULL
THEN *expression_n*
ELSE NULL
END

The next example demonstrates COALESCE by displaying a literal value if student does not have a class code.

```
SELECT  last_name
        ,COALESCE(class_code, 'Missing Class') AS Class_code
FROM    student_table
ORDER BY class_code;

Result: 10 rows returned

Last_name                   Class_code
--------------------        -------------
Johnson                     Missing Class
Garrett                     FR
Kojack                      FR
Lamp                        FR
Rieter                      JR
Bond                        JR
McCann                      SO
McCormick                   SO
Phillips                    SR
Craig                       SR
```

Figure 13.5

The Teradata extension, ZEROIFNULL, can only test one argument and can only return a zero, or the argument.

ZEROIFNULL(*arg*)

It is the equivalent of the following CASE statement:

CASE WHEN *arg* IS NULL
     THEN 0
     ELSE *arg*
END

Practice Questions

1. Identify the illegal CASE statement.
   a. CASE col3 WHEN 3 THEN 'OK' ELSE "Error' END
   b. CASE WHEN col3 = 3 THEN 'OK' ELSE 'Error' END
   c. CASE col3 WHEN col3 = 3 THEN 'OK' ELSE 'Error' END

2. Nested CASE statements are illegal.
   a. TRUE
   b. FALSE

3. COALESCE returns:
   a. The first non-null value.
   b. The last non-null value.
   c. NULL if all arguments evaluate to null.

4. ZEROIFNULL is a Teradata extension.
   a. TRUE
   b. FALSE

5. What will the following query return?
   SELECT COALESCE(NULL, Null, 'null', 'abc', 'defg', NULL);
   a. defg
   b. NULL
   c. abc
   d. null
   e. Null

Chapter Notes

Utilize this space for notes, key points to remember, diagrams, areas of further study, etc.

_____

_____

_____

_____

_____

_____

_____

_____

_____

_____

_____

_____

_____

Chapter 14: View and Macro Processing

Certification Objectives

- ✓ Identify uses of simple and parameterized macros.
- ✓ Identify the benefits of using views and macros.
- ✓ Identify the restrictions of creating views and macros.
- ✓ Describe the impact of using a locking modifier in a view or macro.

Before You Begin

You should be familiar with the following terms and concepts.

Terms	Key Concepts
Views	Reasons to use and considerations along with understanding CREATE, and DROP statements
Locking	Knowledge on how to apply with Views
Macros	Reason to use and considerations along with understanding CREATE, and DROP statements

Views

Views are an essential component to include when establishing or adding to your database schema. Here are some definitions, advantages, recommendations, and restrictions about views.

Definitions

- A view is a virtual table.
- A view may define a subset of rows of a table.
- A view may define a subset of columns of a table.

- Data is neither duplicated nor stored separately for a view.
- View definitions are stored in the Data Dictionary, not in the user's own space.
- Views can simplify the joins of multiple tables into a single virtual table
- Views can act as aggregated tables, where the aggregate data (sum, average etc) is presented as the calculated results.
- Views can provide security by limiting the exposure of a table or tables to users accessing the data.

Advantages

- Provide an additional level of security/authorization.
- Can prevent the end user from missing join conditions
- Help control read and update privileges
- Are not affected if columns are added to a table.
- Are not affected if a column is dropped from a table unless the dropped column is referenced by the view
- Simplify end-user access

Recommendations

- Only utilities, such as FastLoad, MultiLoad, Tpump, and Teradata Parallel Transporter (TPT) should have direct access to the base tables. All other access should be done through views
- Create at least one view for each base table
- Create for commonly used business analytics.

Restrictions

- A view cannot contain an ORDER BY clause.
- The WHERE clause of a SELECT against a view can reference all aggregated columns of that view.

- Derived columns and aggregate columns must have an AS clause.
- A view cannot be used to UPDATE if it contains:
  - Data from more than one table (JOIN VIEW)
  - The same column twice
  - Derived columns
  - A DISTINCT clause
  - A GROUP BY clause

Creating a View

The CREATE VIEW command defines a view. As discussed, a view is not physically created. Its definition is simply stored in the Data Dictionary. By design, Teradata will generate a query rewrite to support the retrieve operation of a view. To CREATE a full-table VIEW, do the following:

CREATE VIEW dept AS SELECT * FROM department_table;

To see a view definition, do the following:

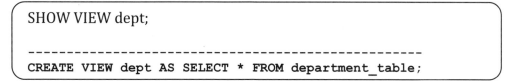

```
SHOW VIEW dept;

-----------------------------------------------------
CREATE VIEW dept AS SELECT * FROM department_table;
```

Figure 14.1

The SHOW VIEW command only returns the original text. Therefore, it is recommended that all views be created with explicit column names in the SELECT statement.

When the view is created, the * will be expanded to the complete list of column names in the table. To see all of the columns in a view, do the following:

HELP VIEW dept:

Figure 14.2

Adding columns to a table does not affect or change any views referencing the table. Dropping a column from a table will render any view referencing the dropped column unusable. Views may not contain an ORDER BY unless they contain a TOP TEN WITH TIES.

The following is an example of the recommended way for creating a view by explicitly listing the columns. The users will see and use the column names supplied inside the parentheses.

```
CREATE VIEW  Employee_Dept_200_V
(Emp_Nbr, LAST, Salary)
AS  SELECT  employee_no
          ,last_name
          ,salary
   FROM   employee_table
   WHERE  dept_no = 200;
```

Figure 14.3

Using a View

As stated above, the SHOW VIEW returns the CREATE VIEW text. Here is an example.

```
SHOW VIEW employee_dept_200_V ;

CREATE VIEW  Employee_Dept_200_V
(Emp_Nbr, LAST, Salary)
AS   SELECT   employee_no
             ,last_name
             ,salary
    FROM    employee_table
    WHERE   dept_no = 200;
```

Figure 14.4

The name of a view is used in constructing SQL, just like using a table name. Here is the result of doing a query using the above view.

```
SELECT * FROM employee_dept_200_V ;

Result: 2 rows returned

    Emp_Nbr  LAST                    Salary
  -----------  --------------------   ----------
    1333454  Roberts                 48800.00
    1324657  Willis                  42788.88
```

Figure 14.5

LOCKING Request Modifier

When a view is defined with a LOCKING modifier, the specified lock is placed on the underlying base table set each time the view is referenced in an SQL statement.

A LOCKING modifier that specifies locking for ACCESS can be used in a CREATE VIEW statement to give concurrent access for end/business users and data integration processes that will modify the data. This is the recommended approach.

The default READ lock caused by the SELECT statement in a view can be overridden by placing a LOCKING FOR ACCESS modifier on the view. An ACCESS lock allows data to be retrieved during write activities. Be aware that a view defined with an ACCESS lock might display inconsistent results.

```
CREATE VIEW Read_to_Access AS
(LOCKING sales_table FOR ACCESS
  SELECT * FROM sales_table);
```

Figure 14.6

Since this is an updatable view, the system will automatically upgrade the lock to a WRITE lock if the view is used to modify the sales_table.

Macro Processing

Macros are a Teradata extension. The following lists important attributes of macros.

Definitions

- Macros contain one or more prewritten SQL statements.
- Macros are a Teradata extension to ANSI SQL.
- Macros are stored in the Teradata Data Dictionary.

- Macros can be executed from any viable SQL front-end, including:
    - SQL Assistant
    - BTEQ
    - Preprocessor
    - CLI
    - LOGON Startup
    - Another macro

Advantages

- Users only need the EXEC privilege to run a macro.
- No underlying table or view privileges are required to EXECute a macro.
- Macros are executed as a single transaction. All SQL within a macro must successfully complete or any changes will be backed out.
- Macros can provide column-level security.
- Macros can be parameterized.
- Macros are a good method for encapsulating business logic
    - Reusability: Can re-used (less repetitive code writing)
    - Single Set of Code: Ensures that a standardized set of logic is utilized (reduces likelihood of having "bad logic" or "stale" SQL, if everyone is using the same logic).

Restrictions

- The macro creator must have the necessary permissions to accomplish the SQL statements within a macro.
- The *macroname* must be a unique *objectname* within the database it resides.
- Every SQL statement in a macro must end with a semicolon.

- Nonqualified names in a macro definition are *not* resolved in DDL statements when the macro is created. They are not resolved until the macro is performed.
- Nonqualified names in a macro definition are *fully* resolved in DML statements when the macro is created.
- There cannot be more than one DDL statement in a macro, and it must be the last statement.

The following chart lists the SQL commands associated with macros.

Macro-related Commands

COMMAND	DEFINITION
CREATE MACRO macroname AS (...);	Define a macro and store it the Data Dictionary.
REPLACE MACRO macroname AS (...);	Modify an existing macro. If the referenced macro does not exist, a new macro will be created.
EXECute macroname;	Execute the statements within the macro.
SHOW MACRO macroname;	Display a macro.
DROP MACRO macroname;	Remove a macro definition from the Data Dictionary
EXPLAIN EXEC macroname;	Display EXPLAIN text for the macro's execution.

Figure 14.7

Here is a macro to report employee job assignments:

```
CREATE MACRO EmpJob AS
( SELECT
  TRIM(last_name) || ', ' || TRIM(first_name) AS Employee
, TRIM(job_desc) AS JobTitle
FROM employee_table e
JOIN
emp_job_table  ej
ON e.employee_no = ej.emp_no
JOIN
job_table  j
ON ej.job_no = j.job_no
ORDER BY last_name;
);
```

Figure 14.8

Once a macros has been created, you run it by using the EXEC command, as shown below.

```
EXEC empjob;

Result: 8 rows returned

Employee                            JobTitle
----------------------------------  --------------------
Clooney, George                     Programmer
Ford, Harrison                      Manager
Gere, Richard                       Developer
Roberts, Julia                      Security Guard
Strickland, Stan                    Programmer
Student, Mandee                     Developer
Travolta, John                      Project Manager
Willis, Bruce                       Programmer
```

Figure 14.9

Here is another macro to show the students who are currently enrolled in classes:

```
CREATE MACRO enrollments AS
(SELECT
  last_name
  ,first_name
  ,sc.course_id
  ,course_name
FROM   student_table AS s
INNER JOIN
  Student_course_table AS sc
ON   s.student_id = sc.student_id
INNER JOIN
  Course_table c
ON   sc.course_id = c.course_id
ORDER BY sc.course_id, last_name;
);
```

Figure 14.10

Now, whenever anyone wants that report, all they
the macro. The following is the example.

```
EXEC enrollments;

Result: 13 rows returned

Last_name              First_name    Course_ID Course_name
--------------------   -----------   --------- ------------------------------
Garrett                Wendy              100 Teradata Basics
Kojack                 Henry              100 Teradata Basics
Phillips               Beth               100 Teradata Basics
Craig                  Danny              200 Introduction to SQL
Kojack                 Henry              200 Introduction to SQL
McCormick              Susie              210 Advanced SQL
Rieter                 Richard            210 Advanced SQL
Bond                   Jimmy              220 TD12 SQL Features
Kojack                 Henry              220 TD12 SQL Features
McCormick              Susie              220 TD12 SQL Features
Bond                   Jimmy              300 Physical Database Tuning
Johnson                Stephen            400 Database Administration
McCann                 Andy               400 Database Administration
```

Figure 14.11

So, for canned reports like this, macros simplify life for the users.

Parameterized Macros

If you want to vary the results produced by a macro, Teradata macros
can accept parameter values for data values. The syntax for creating a
macro with parameters is:

CREATE | REPLACE MACRO macroname
(parametername datatype [, parametername datatype . . .]
AS
(<SQL statements>) ;

To reference a parameter within an SQL statement, precede the
parameter name with a colon (:). Here is an example of a

rameterized macro to show which employees have a specific job
code:

```
CREATE MACRO JobEmp (jobcode INT) AS
( SELECT
  TRIM(last_name) || ', ' || TRIM(first_name) AS Employee
, ej.Job_no AS JobCode
, TRIM(job_desc) AS JobTitle
FROM employee_table e
JOIN
emp_job_table ej
ON e.employee_no = ej.emp_no
JOIN
job_table j
ON ej.job_no = :jobcode
AND  ej.job_no = j.job_no
ORDER BY last_name;
);
```

Figure 14.12

The following shows running the macro and the result:

```
EXEC jobemp ( 20010 );


Result: 3 rows returned

Employee                             JobCode  JobTitle
-----------------------------------  -------  --------------------
Clooney, George                        20010  Programmer
Strickland, Stan                       20010  Programmer
Willis, Bruce                          20010  Programmer
```

Figure 14.13

Parameter Restrictions

When using parameters, you cannot pass the names of database objects in a macro as a parameter. Database objects refer to databases / tables / views and their columns. In addition, the following data attributes are never valid with macro parameters:

- CHECK constraints
- FROM statements cannot be parameterized
- COMPRESS phrase

Practice Questions

1. Macros must have parameters.
    a. TRUE
    b. FALSE

2. Non-qualified DDL names in macros:
    a. Are fully resolved when the macro is created.
    b. Are fully resolved when the macro is executed.

3. Non-qualified DML names in macros:
    a. Are fully resolved when the macro is created.
    b. Are fully resolved when the macro is executed.

4. Choose the correct ending for the following statement.
   Each statement in a macro_____
    a. Must end with a semicolon.
    b. Is treated as a transaction.

5. To see the expanded list of column names from CV v1 AS SEL *
   FROM t1;, do the following.
    a. HELP VIEW v1;
    b. SHOW VIEW v1;
    c. EXPLAIN VIEW v1;

6. Choose the correct view definition.
    a. cv v1 as sel c1, c2, avg(c3) from t1;
    b. cv v1 as sel c1, c2, avg(c3) from t1 order by 3;
    c. cv v1 as sel c1, c2, avg(c3) as c3 from t1;

7. Join views are updatable.
    a. TRUE
    b. FALSE

Chapter Notes

Utilize this space for notes, key points to remember, diagrams, areas of further study, etc.

_____

_____

_____

_____

_____

_____

_____

_____

_____

_____

_____

_____

_____

_____

_____

Chapter 15: Transaction Processing

Certification Objectives

✓ List the differences between ANSI and Teradata modes in the areas of transaction protocol, defaults, conversions, and table creation.

✓ Given a set of scenarios, identify which transactions are running in ANSI mode and which are running in Teradata mode.

✓ Describe usage of built-in Teradata functions (i.e. locking modifiers).

Before You Begin

You should be familiar with the following terms and concepts.

Terms	Key Concepts
Transaction Locking	Considerations and restrictions
BTET vs. ANSI	Knowledge on how to apply and the differences
ABORT	How does this work - Teradata vs. ANSI mode

Transactions

Transaction processing is designed to maintain a database in a known, consistent state by ensuring that any operations carried out are interdependent, which means that entire transactions are either completed successfully or canceled successfully.

Transaction processing allows for single or multiple operations. In addition, multiple transactions can be linked together to create a single transaction. In this case, the Teradata Transient Journal ensures that either all operations in a transaction are completed without error, or none of them are. This is accomplished through a series of row and table level locks. If some of the SQL statements are completed but errors occur when the others are attempted, the Transient Journal will rollback all of the operations in the transaction, thereby erasing all traces of the transaction and restoring the system to the consistent, known state that it was in before processing of the transaction began.

If all SQL statements of a transaction are completed successfully, the transaction is committed by the system, and all changes to the database are made permanent; the transaction cannot be rolled back once this is done. Lastly, the Transient Journal will purge the before images upon successful completion of the transaction.

In addition, the Teradata database guards against hardware and software errors that might leave a transaction partially completed with the system left in an unknown, inconsistent state. For example, if the database crashes in the middle of a transaction, the transaction processing system guarantees that all operations in an *uncommitted* state are cancelled and their changes rolled back.

Transaction Locking

Any number of users and applications can simultaneously access data stored in a Teradata database.

The Teradata Database Lock Manager imposes concurrency control by locking the database object being accessed by each transaction and releasing those locks when the transaction either commits or rolls back its work. This control ensures that the data remains consistent for all users.

Locking Levels

Locking levels determine the type of object that is locked and the impact on other users, as follows:

LOCKING LEVEL	Resource(s) unavailable to other users
DATABASE	All tables, views, macros and triggers owned by the database/user.
VIEW	All tables referenced in the View.
TABLE	All rows in the base table and in any secondary index and fallback subtables associated with it.
ROW	The primary copy of rows sharing the same row hash value. A row hash lock permits other users to access other data in the table and is the least restrictive type of automatic lock. A row hash lock applies to a *set* of rows that shares the same hash code. It does not necessarily, nor even generally, lock only one row. • A row hash lock is applied whenever a table is accessed using a *primary index (PI)*. • For an update that uses a *unique secondary index (USI)*, the appropriate row of the secondary index subtable is also locked. • It is not necessary to lock the fallback copy of the row, nor any associated row, of a *nonunique secondary index* (NUSI) subtable.

Figure 15.1

Note: With the exception of pseudo-table locks, locks in the Teradata Database are not managed globally, but by each AMP individually.

Lock Types

The next chart lists the types of locks that can be placed on database objects.

LOCK TYPE	DESCRIPTION
ACCESS	• Permits selection of data from a base table that can be locked for write by other users. • Because the data selected using an ACCESS lock can be inconsistent because the data might be modified concurrently with the request, you should only use this lock for casual inspection of data. • Placing an ACCESS lock requires the SELECT privilege on the specified object.
READ	• Ensures data consistency during a read operation such as a SELECT request. • This is the default lock on SELECT statements. • Multiple users can concurrently hold a READ lock on a base table. As long as a READ lock is in place, no modification of the object is allowed. • Placing a READ lock requires the SELECT privilege on the specified object. • SHARE is a synonym for READ

WRITE	<ul><li>Enables a single user to modify data.</li><li>This is the default for INSERT, UPDATE, and DELETE statements.</li><li>As long as the WRITE lock is in place, all other users are excluded from viewing or modifying the object except readers who are viewing data using an ACCESS lock.</li><li>Until a WRITE lock is released, no new READ locks are permitted on the locked object.</li><li>Placing a WRITE lock requires an UPDATE, INSERT, or DELETE privilege on the specified object.</li></ul>
EXCLUSIVE	<ul><li>Excludes all other users.</li><li>This is the most restrictive lock.</li><li>EXCLUSIVE locks are rarely used except to make structural changes to a database.</li><li>This is the default on all DDL statements.</li><li>Placing an EXCLUSIVE lock on a database object requires the DROP privilege on that object.</li></ul>
CHECKSUM	<ul><li>Used only with updatable cursors in embedded SQL and stored procedures.</li></ul>

Figure 15.2

Lock Queue

When a lock is requested, the system will either Grant the lock, or put the request into the lock Queue as follows.

LOCK HELD	LOCK REQUESTED			
	ACCESS	READ	WRITE	EXCLUSIVE
None	Grant	Grant	Grant	Grant
ACCESS	Grant	Grant	Grant	Queue
READ	Grant	Grant	Queue	Queue
WRITE	Grant	Queue	Queue	Queue
EXCLUSIVE	Queue	Queue	Queue	Queue

Figure 15.3

Notice in the chart above that ACCESS and WRITE locks are compatible.

Any lock can be upgraded, but only a READ lock can be downgraded to an ACCESS lock. Use the LOCKING modifier to change a lock. Here are the syntax formats of the LOCKING Modifier:

LOCKING [<table-name>] FOR <desired-locking> [NOWAIT]
LOCKING ROW FOR <desired-locking> [NOWAIT]
LOCKING DATABASE <database-name> FOR <desired-locking> [NOWAIT]
LOCKING VIEW <view-name> FOR <desired-locking> [NOWAIT]
LOCKING TABLE <table-name> FOR <desired-locking> [NOWAIT]

NOWAIT instructs the system to abort the request if the lock cannot be granted immediately. Specify this option for situations in which it is not desirable to have a request wait for resources, and possibly tie up resources another request could use, while waiting.

Here is an example of the improper use of the LOCKING modifier.

LOCKING ROW FOR READ SELECT * FROM employee_table;

Figure 15.4

Though the request asks for a row hash Read lock, the query does not use either the Primary Index or a USI to access the table. Therefore, the system will ignore the row lock request and apply a full-table Read lock.

Transaction Modes

Here are some terms associated with transaction processing that you should understand:

TERM	DEFINITION
Statement	An SQL command that ends with a semicolon.
Request	One, or more, statements sent to the Parser for execution.
Transaction	One, or more, requests that take the database from one consistent state to another consistent state.

Figure 15.5

Teradata performs transaction processing in either of the following modes:

- ANSI
- Teradata

In ANSI mode, transaction processing adheres to the rules defined by the ANSI SQL specification. In Teradata mode, transaction processing follows the rules defined by Teradata. Below are a few comparisons between the two modes.

Comparison Chart

TERADATA Mode	ANSI Mode
Data comparison is **not case specific**. Character literal values can be coded in SQL as lower case or upper case. The search engine would view an 'A' the same as an 'a' and data would be returned.	Data comparison is **case specific**. Character literal values must be coded using the correct case in order for the search engine to determine a match. An 'A' is different than an 'a' and data would not be returned.

Allows truncation of displayed data. Certain SQL commands covered in earlier chapters allow the user to request less characters be returned than the number of characters stored in a column. This is perfectly acceptable.	**Forbids truncation** of display data. Any attempt to return less than all the data stored in a column will cause the SQL to fail with an error (3996).
A transaction is **implicit** by nature – each SQL statement is a stand-alone transaction and the work committed upon a successful completion. A transaction can also be **explicit** with a BEGIN TRANSACTION (BT) command and an END TRANSACTION (ET) command. The presence of the ET command will cause all successfully completed SQL work to be committed and make it permanent.	All transactions are **explicit only** and at the end of a transaction a COMMIT WORK command is required in order to commit all successfully completed work and make it permanent.
The **CREATE TABLE** will default to: **SET** table (no duplicate rows allowed). Non-case specific character data columns.	The **CREATE TABLE** will default to: **MULTISET** table (duplicate rows allowed). Case specific character data columns.

Figure 15.6

Setting the Transaction Mode

The default mode in Teradata is Teradata mode, which is set at the system level. To set the transaction processing mode, use the:

- SessionMode field of the DBS Control Record
- Preprocessor2 TRANSACT() option
- BTEQ command .SET SESSION TRANSACTION (shown below)

```
-- set transaction mode to Teradata
.SET SESSION TRANSACTION BTET;

or

-- set transaction mode to ANSI
.SET SESSION TRANSACTION ANSI;
```

Figure 15.7

Teradata Mode Transactions

Locks are acquired up front when users execute other requests using the same tables. These request types are also considered implicit transactions (or system-generated transactions). Therefore, the system holds locks for these request types until the requests complete.

- Multi-statement only DML requests
- Single statement DDL or DML requests
- Macro multi-statement or single statement requests

The table-level write locks needed in these requests are:

- Acquired in TableID order
- Held until done

This minimizes deadlocks at the table level when many users execute requests on the same tables.

Transaction Semantics - BTET Mode

The following discusses the difference between implicit and explicit transactions and how they are handled in BT/ET transaction mode.

Implicit transaction
- Each SQL request is an implicit transaction by default
- Each failed request is automatically rolled back.

Explicit transaction
- Launched with explicit BEGIN TRANSACTION (BT)

Ended explicitly by:
- END TRANSACTION (ET)—commit work done since BT
- ROLLBACK—rollback work done since BT

Ended implicitly by:
- Any request failure—rollback work done since BT

Here are examples for you to study.

Implicit Transaction	Explicit Transaction
.LOGON INSERT row1; (txn#1) INSERT row2; (txn#2) .LOGOFF	BT; (txn#1) INSERT row1; INSERT row2; ET;
Two transactions. Failure of one doesn't affect the other.	One transaction. Failure of one will rollback to BT.

Figure 15.8

ANSI Mode Transactions

Apart from transaction semantics, you can write SQL code with explicit specifications to override defaults so that it performs identically in both ANSI and Teradata modes. The following rules are enforced in ANSI mode.

A transaction initiation is always *implicit*. A transaction is opened by the first SQL statement executed in a session or by the first statement executed following the close of a transaction. The COMMIT [WORK] or ROLLBACK [WORK] statements close a transaction.

In ANSI mode, the user must commit the work to disk in order to save the work. The COMMIT WORK; command must be used to successfully end an ANSI transaction (single or multi-step command):

To perform this statement in BTEQ - ANSI mode, the following can be used:

```
UPDATE Employee_Table
SET  Salary = Salary * 1.1
WHERE Employee_No = 1232578 ;
.if errorcode > 0  then .quit  ERRORCODE
UPDATE  Department_Table   FROM Employee_Table  AS  E
SET  Budget_Amount = Budget_Amount + (Salary * .01)
WHERE  E.Dept_No = Department_Table.Dept_no
AND      E.Employee_no = 1232578 ;
COMMIT WORK ;
```

Figure 15.9

Note: In Teradata (BTET) mode, the COMMIT WORK is not required.

Transaction Semantics - ANSI Mode

All transactions in ANSI mode are explicit. The following discusses ANSI explicit transactions and how they are handled.

Explicit transaction
- Transaction is launched with first SQL request.
- All transactions are explicitly ended.
- Transaction ended explicitly by:
    - COMMIT WORK—commit work done since launch
    - ROLLBACK—rollback work done since launch

The following chart summarizes this.

No Explicit Ending	Explicit Ending
.LOGON INSERT row1; (txn#1) INSERT row2; .LOGOFF	.LOGON INSERT row1; (txn#1) INSERT row2; COMMIT WORK; .LOGOFF
One transaction. LOGOFF without COMMIT – both INSERTs roll back.	One transaction. Failure of either has no effect on the other. COMMIT commits successful requests only.

Figure 15.10

Aborting Transactions

The other way to end a transaction besides either ET; or COMMIT WORK;, is to use either the ABORT or ROLLBACK statement. The syntax for the ABORT/ROLLBACK statement is:

ABORT | ROLLBACK ['abort_message'] [FROM_clause]
[WHERE_clause] ;

SYNTAX ELEMENT	DESCRIPTION
ABORT ROLLBACK	ABORT is a Teradata extension to the ANSI SQL-2003 standard.
'abort_message'	The text of the message to be returned when the transaction is terminated.
FROM_clause	Only required if the WHERE_clause includes a subquery.
WHERE_clause	• An optional clause that specifies an expression whose result must evaluate to TRUE if the transaction is to be rolled back. • If the result of the WHERE_clause evaluates to FALSE, then transaction processing continues. • If you do not specify a WHERE_clause, then rollback occurs unconditionally. • The abort condition described by the WHERE_clause can also specify an aggregate operation.

Figure 15.11

Note: In ANSI mode, if a user logs off without performing a COMMIT command, Teradata will consider this an aborted transaction and all work will be rolled back.

Practice Questions

1. Choose the BTEQ command to change from BT/ET to ANSI mode.
    a. .SET SESSION MODE ANSI;
    b. .SET SESSION TRANSACTION ANSI;
    c. .SET SESSION TRANSACTION MODE ANSI;

2. In ANSI mode, the default table kind is:
    a. SET
    b. MULTISET

3. A Write lock can be downgraded to a Read lock.
    a. TRUE
    b. FALSE

4. An Access lock request will be blocked by:
    a. Another Access lock.
    b. A Read lock.
    c. A Write lock.
    d. An Exclusive lock.

5. If a lock cannot be immediately granted, the NOWAIT option will cause:
    a. The request to queue.
    b. The request to continue processing.
    c. The request to abort.

6. The default lock for SELECT statements is:
   a. Access
   b. Read
   c. Write
   d. Exclusive

7. Locking a view locks all of the tables and views referenced in the view.
   a. TRUE
   b. FALSE

8. The COMMIT WORK; command only commits successfully completed requests.
   a. TRUE
   b. FALSE

Chapter Notes

Utilize this space for notes, key points to remember, diagrams, areas of further study, etc.

_____

_____

_____

_____

_____

_____

_____

_____

_____

_____

_____

_____

_____

_____

Chapter 16: Data Definition Language

Certification Objectives

✓ Given a CREATE TABLE statement without a primary index declared, identify the column that Teradata will select as the primary index.
✓ Describe the characteristics of MLPPI and PPI tables.
✓ Identify the functionality Queue Tables, Table functions, and Triggers.
✓ Identify the effect of dropping or altering a partition.
✓ Describe the attributes and constraints for a column in a table.
✓ Given a scenario, identify considerations using a CREATE TABLE AS definition.

Before You Begin

You should be familiar with the following terms and concepts.

Terms	Key Concepts
CREATE TABLE	Considerations, options, and restrictions
Table Attributes	Understand the types and how to utilize
PPI / MLPPI	Knowledge on how to apply and the differences

Data Definition Language (DDL) is used to create, modify, and remove object definitions. This chapter will discuss DDL in respect to Tables, Indexes, and Triggers.

CREATE TABLE

The CREATE TABLE statement can be broken down into four major areas as seen in the syntax example and chart below.

CREATE TABLE Syntax

CREATE [SET/MULTISET] [VOLATILE/GLOBAL TEMPORARY]
TABLE tablename
        <Create Table Options>
        <Column Definitions>
        <Table-level Constraints>
        <Index Definitions>;

Where:

Create Table options	Specify physical attributes of table: Fallback Journaling Freespace Datablocksize

Column definitions	Define each column's data type, attributes, and any constraints:
	  o PRIMARY KEY
	  o UNIQUE
	  o CHECK
	  o REFERENCES
	or GENERATED

Table-level constraints	Define multi-column constraints: PRIMARY KEY FOREIGN KEY UNIQUE CHECK conditions
Index definitions	Specify indexes for physical access to data
Row retention	COMMIT options

Figure 16.1

SET/MULTISET - Duplicate row option

- SET – no duplicate rows allowed. This is the Teradata session default. If there is no UNIQUE declaration, the system will compare a new row to every table row having the same row hash. This is the Teradata session default.
- MULTISET – duplicate rows allowed. Multiset tables exist outside of the relational model, since relational tables must have a Primary Key. This is the ANSI session default.

Table type options

- Permanent – This is the default.
- VOLATILE – exists only for the duration of the user's session
- GLOBAL TEMPORARY– definition is permanent, but data exists only for the duration of the user's session

Table protection options

- [NO] FALLBACK PROTECTION
- [NO] LOG
- [NO|DUAL] BEFORE JOURNAL
- [NO|DUAL|LOCAL|[NOT] LOCAL] AFTER JOURNAL
- FREESPACE = n [PERCENT] (percentage of cylinder freespace)
- DATABLOCKSIZE = n BYTES (maximum data block size)

Column names

Column names must be unique within the table.

Column data type

Refer to Chapter 4 for the list of data types.

Data Type Attributes

DEFAULT <value>	Specify a default value in place of a null
WITH DEFAULT	Specify the use of a system default value in place of a null
DEFAULT USER DEFAULT DATE DEFAULT TIME DEFAULT NULL	Insert username of the session Insert CURRENT_DATE Insert CURRENT_TIME Insert a null
FORMAT	Default display format
TITLE	Default column title
NAMED	Default name
UPPERCASE	Shift to uppercase for storage
CASESPECIFIC	Store as entered

Figure 16.2

Column-Level Constraints

Column-level constraints may be unnamed. If named, each name must be unique. Named constraint names must adhere to normal naming restrictions.

UNIQUE	The column must be NOT NULL and not allow duplicates
PRIMARY KEY	The column must be NOT NULL and not allow duplicates
CHECK (boolean condition)	Cannot reference other columns
REFERENCES [WITH [NO]] CHECK OPTION tablename (columnname)	The WITH CHECK OPTION will implement full referential integrity

Figure 16.3

Storage Attributes

COMPRESS	Nulls will be compressed to zero space.
COMPRESS NULL	Nulls will be compressed to zero space.
COMPRESS (<value_list>)	Nulls and the constant(s) will be compressed to zero space.

Figure 16.4

Table Naming Conventions

Names are 1 to 30 characters in length and may only include the following characters:

- Uppercase or lowercase letters (A to Z and a to z)
- Digits (0 through 9)
- The special characters DOLLAR SIGN ($), NUMBER SIGN (#), and LOW LINE (_) a.k.a. UNDERSCORE
- They must not begin with a digit.
- They must not be a reserved word.

Names that define databases and objects must observe the following rules.

- Databases, users, and profiles must have unique names within the system.
- Tables, views, stored procedures, join or hash indexes, triggers, user-defined functions, and macros must have unique names within a database or user.
- Table and view columns must have unique names within the table or view.
- Parameters defined for a macro or stored procedure must have unique names.
- Secondary indexes which are assigned names must have names that are unique to the table.

- Constraints on a table, which are assigned names, must have names that are unique to the table.
- CHECK constraints, REFERENCE constraints, and INDEX objects can also have *assigned* names. Names are optional for these objects.
- Names are not case-specific

ANSI standards state that indexes on a table are optional. However, Teradata requires a Primary Index for distributing rows across the AMPs. If no Primary Index is declared when a table is created, Teradata will make the first column a Non-Unique Primary Index (NUPI) as the illustrations below demonstrate.

Teradata table creation syntax is illustrated below:

```
CREATE TABLE emp_data
        (employee_number   INTEGER       NOT NULL
        ,user_name         CHAR(25)      DEFAULT USER
        ,last_name         CHAR(20)      NOT NULL
                                         WITH DEFAULT
        ,street_address    VARCHAR(30)   TITLE 'Address'
        ,city              CHAR(15)      DEFAULT 'Santa Clara'
        ,state             CHAR(2)       WITH DEFAULT
        ,birthdate         DATE          FORMAT 'mm/dd/yy'
        ,salary_amount     DEC(10,2)
        ,sex               CHAR(1)       UPPERCASE
                                         COMPRESS ('M', 'F')  );
```

Figure 16.5

Teradata 12 Certification Study Guide

Teradata table implementation syntax shown in the next example:

```
CREATE SET TABLE CSQL_CLASS.emp_data ,NO FALLBACK ,
     NO BEFORE JOURNAL,
     NO AFTER JOURNAL,
     CHECKSUM = DEFAULT
     (employee_number INTEGER NOT NULL,
      user_name CHAR(25) CHARACTER SET LATIN
                         NOT CASESPECIFIC
                         DEFAULT USER,
      last_name CHAR(20) CHARACTER SET LATIN
                         NOT CASESPECIFIC
                         NOT NULL
                         DEFAULT '                    ',
      street_address VARCHAR(30) CHARACTER SET LATIN
                         NOT CASESPECIFIC
                         TITLE 'Address',
      city CHAR(15) CHARACTER SET LATIN
                         NOT CASESPECIFIC
                         DEFAULT 'Santa Clara    ',
      state CHAR(2) CHARACTER SET LATIN
                         NOT CASESPECIFIC
                         DEFAULT '  ',
      birthdate DATE FORMAT 'mm/dd/yy',
      salary_amount DECIMAL(10,2),
      sex CHAR(1) CHARACTER SET LATIN
                         UPPERCASE
                         NOT CASESPECIFIC
                         COMPRESS ('F','M'))
PRIMARY INDEX ( employee_number );
```

Figure 16.6

Note: More on this topic will be covered later in the chapter.

Referential Integrity

Referencing (Child) Table

The referencing table is referred to as the child table, and the specified child table columns are the referencing columns.

Referenced (Parent) Table

A child table must have a parent, and the referenced table is referred to as the parent table. The parent key columns in the parent table are the referenced columns. Because the referenced columns are always defined as unique, they must be implemented as one of the following unique indexes:

- A unique primary index (UPI), defined as NOT NULL
- A unique secondary index (USI), defined as NOT NULL

Rules for Assigning Columns as Foreign Keys

The FOREIGN KEY columns in the *referencing* table must be identical in definition with the keys in the *referenced* table. Corresponding columns must have the same data type and case sensitivity.
- The COMPRESS option is not permitted on either the referenced or referencing column(s).
- Column level constraints are not compared.
- A one-column FOREIGN KEY cannot reference a single column in a multicolumn primary or unique key—the foreign and primary/unique key must contain the same number of columns.

Circular References Are Allowed

References can be defined as circular in that TableA can reference TableB, which can reference TableA. In this case, at least one set of FOREIGN KEYS must be defined on nullable columns.

If the FOREIGN KEYS in TableA are on columns defined as nullable, then rows could be inserted into TableA with nulls for the FOREIGN KEY columns. Once the appropriate rows exist in TableB, the nulls of the FOREIGN KEY columns in TableA could then be updated to contain non-null values which match the TableB values.

References Can Be to the Table Itself

FOREIGN KEY references can also be to the same table that contains the FOREIGN KEY. The referenced columns must be different columns than the FOREIGN KEY, and both the referenced and referencing columns must subscribe to the referential integrity rules.

Maintaining Foreign Keys

Definition of a FOREIGN KEY requires that the Teradata Database maintain the integrity defined between the *referenced* and *referencing* table.

The Teradata Database maintains the integrity of foreign keys as explained in the following table.

For this data manipulation activity ...	The system verifies that ...
A row is inserted into a *referencing* table and foreign key columns are defined to be NOT NULL.	a row exists in the *referenced* table with the same values as those in the foreign key columns.

	If such a row does not exist, then an error is returned. If the foreign key contains multiple columns, and if any one column value of the foreign key is null, then none of the foreign key values are validated.
The values in foreign key columns are altered to be NOT NULL.	a row exists in the *referenced* table that contains values equal to the altered values of all of the foreign key columns. If such a row does not exist, then an error is returned.
A row is deleted from a *referenced* table.	no rows exist in *referencing* tables with foreign key values equal to those of the row to be deleted. If such rows exist, then an error is returned.
Before a *referenced* column in a *referenced* table is updated.	no rows exist in a referencing table with foreign key values equal to those of the referenced columns. If such rows exist, then an error is returned.
Before the structure of columns defined as foreign keys or referenced by foreign keys is altered.	the change would not violate the rules for definition of a foreign key constraint. An ALTER TABLE or DROP INDEX statement attempting to change such a columns structure returns

	an error.
A table *referenced* by another is dropped.	the referencing table has dropped its foreign key reference to the referenced table.

An ALTER TABLE statement adds a foreign key reference to a table.	all of the values in the foreign key columns are validated against columns in the referenced table.
	
	When the system parses ALTER TABLE, it defines an error table that:
	• Has the same columns and primary index as the target table of the ALTER TABLE statement.
	• Has a name that is the same as the target table name suffixed with the reference index number. A reference index number is assigned to each foreign key constraint for a table.
	To determine the number, use one of the following system views.
	    o RI_Child_Tables
	    o RI_Distinct_Children
	    o RI_Distinct_Parents
	    o RI_Parent_Tables
	• Is created under the same user or database as the table being altered.
	
	If a table already exists with the same name as that generated for the error table then an error is returned to the ALTER TABLE

| | statement.

Rows in the referencing table that contain values in the foreign key columns that cannot be found in any row of the referenced table are copied into the error table (the base data of the target table is not modified).

It is your responsibility to:
• Correct data values in the referenced or referencing tables so that full referential integrity exists between the two tables. Use the rows in the error table to define which corrections to make.
• Maintain the error table. |
|---|---|

Figure 16.7

Here is an example:

```
CREATE TABLE customer_table
(customer_number INTEGER NOT NULL PRIMARY KEY
,customer_name VARCHAR(20)
,phone_number CHAR(8)
)
INDEX (Customer_name)
INDEX (Phone_number);
```

Figure 16.8

Notice how the Primary Key has been implemented as a Unique Primary Index.

```
CREATE TABLE order_table
(order_number INTEGER NOT NULL
,customer_number INTEGER NOT NULL
 CONSTRAINT cust_fk REFERENCES WITH CHECK OPTION
customer_table (customer_number)
,order_date DATE FORMAT 'YY/MM/DD'
,order_total DECIMAL(10,2)
)
UNIQUE PRIMARY INDEX (Order_Number)
INDEX (Customer_number)
INDEX (Order_Date);
```

Figure 16.9

Multi-column constraints can only be declared as table-level constraints, after the final column declaration.

```
CREATE SET TABLE CSQL_CLASS.emp_job_table
  ( job_no INTEGER NOT NULL,
   emp_no INTEGER NOT NULL,
   PRIMARY KEY (job_no, emp_no))
PRIMARY INDEX ( job_no );

SHOW TABLE CSQL_CLASS.emp_job_table;
```

Figure 16.10

INDEX definitions

A CREATE TABLE may specify
- A Primary Index
- A Primary Key

- Both
- Neither

Primary Key vs. Primary Index

A Primary Index is different from a primary key in that its values can change, and that its purpose is not for row identification, but for data distribution.

The Primary Index is often, but not necessarily the same column(s) as the primary key. This is because the Primary Index is designed to be the best physical path to the data, whereas the primary key is intended to be the best logical path to the data. The Primary Index, by design, maximizes performance and accessibility. The following illustrates the key differences between the Primary Key and Primary Index.

Primary Key
- One or more columns used to uniquely identify the rows in a table
- Used in conjunction with foreign keys to define the important column relationships in a database
- Always unique and cannot be null
- Not known to the Teradata RDBMS as keys

Primary Index
- One or more columns used to distribute and locate the rows in a table.
- Choice of primary index will affect distribution, access and thus performance.
- Indexes (primary or secondary) may be used to enforce uniqueness.
- Indexes (primary or secondary) may be used to improve access.

- Indexes (primary or secondary) may be unique or non-unique.

Depending on how you choose to count them, the Teradata Database supports between ten and twenty index types:

- Unique non-partitioned primary
- Non-unique non-partitioned primary
- Single-level unique partitioned primary
- Multilevel unique partitioned primary
- Single-level non-unique non-partitioned primary
- Multilevel non-unique partitioned primary
- Join
  A join index composed of virtual rows, with multiple fixed column sets appended to single repeating column set is said to be compressed.
  - Compressed
  - Non-compressed
  Whether compressed or non-compressed, a join index can be any of the following types:
  - Multi-table simple
  - Multi-table aggregate
  - Multi-table sparse
  - Single-table simple
  - Single-table aggregate
  - Single-table sparse
- Hash
- Unique secondary
- Non-unique secondary
  - Hash-ordered on all columns with ALL option
  - Hash-ordered on single column with ALL option
  - Value-ordered on single column with ALL option
  - Hash-ordered on all columns without ALL option
  - Hash-ordered on single column without ALL option
  - Value-ordered on single column without ALL option

The following chart shows the strengths and possible drawbacks of the various indexing methods provided by Teradata.

This access method ...	Has the following strengths ...	And the following possible drawbacks ...
Unique Primary Index (UPI)	• is the most efficient access method when the SQL statement contains the PI value • involves one AMP and one row • requires no spool file (for a simple SELECT) • can obtain the most granular locks	none, in the context of a SELECT statement specifying a PI value. However, a poorly chosen PI can cause poor overall performance in a large workload.
Non-Unique Primary Index (NUPI)	• provides efficient access when the SQL statement contains the PI value • involves one AMP • can obtain granular locks • may not require a spool file as long as the number of rows returned is small	• may slow down INSERTs for a SET table with no USIs. • may decrease the efficiency of SELECTs containing the PI value when some values are repeated in many rows.
Unique Secondary Index (USI)	• provides efficient access when the SQL statement contains the USI values, and you do not specify PI values • involves two AMPs and one row • requires no spool file (for a simple SELECT)	• requires additional overhead for INSERTs, UPDATEs, MERGEs, and DELETEs.
Non-Unique Secondary Index	• provides efficient access when the number of rows per value in the table is	• requires additional overhead for INSERTs, UPDATEs, MERGEs, and

(NUSI)	relatively small • involves all AMPS and probably multiple rows • provides access using information that may be more readily available than a UPI value, such as employee last name, compared to an employee number • may require a spool file	DELETEs. • will not be used by the Optimizer if the number of data blocks accessed is a significant percentage of the data blocks in the table because the Optimizer will determine that a full table scan is cheaper.
Full table scan	• accesses each row only once • provides access using any arbitrary set of column conditions	• examines every row. • usually requires a spool file possibly as large as the base table.
Multi-table Join Index (JI)	• can eliminate the need to perform certain joins and aggregates repetitively • may be able to satisfy a query without referencing the base tables • can have a different PI from that of the base table • can replace a NUSI or a USI	• requires additional overhead for INSERTs, UPDATEs, MERGEs, and DELETEs for any of the base tables that contribute to the multi-table JI. • usually is not suitable for data in tables subjected to a large number of daily INSERTs, UPDATEs, MERGEs, and DELETEs. • imposes some restrictions on operations performed on the base table.
Single-table join index	• Can be used for multiple purposes including:	• requires additional overhead for INSERTs,

(JI) or hash index	• Hash redistribution on non-index columns for join improvement • Sparse indexes • Aggregate indexes • Covered indexes	UPDATEs, MERGEs, and DELETEs. • imposes some restrictions on operations performed on the base table.

Figure 16.11

Secondary and HASH indexes can be added to a table by using the CREATE INDEX and CREATE HASH INDEX commands.

CREATE TABLE AS

Use the CREATE TABLE AS command to create a new table from the results of a query. Syntax for the CREATE TABLE AS is:

CREATE [TEMPORARY | TEMP] TABLE <tablename>
[(<column_name> [, ...])]
AS <select_clause> [Primary Index (<column-list>)]
WITH [NO] DATA;

The example below illustrates a CREATE TABLE AS function:

CREATE TABLE order_table_new AS (SELECT * from order_table)
WITH DATA ;

Figure 16.12

Altering a Table

Through the ALTER TABLE [*databasename.*] *tablename* command, you can:

ADD/MODIFY	FALLBACK
ADD/MODIFY	BEFORE/AFTER journaling
ADD/MODIFY	CHECKSUM
ADD/MODIFY	FREESPACE
ADD/MODIFY	DATABLOCKSIZE
ADD/DROP/RENAME	Columns
ADD/DROP	FOREIGN KEY constraints
DROP	INCONSISTENT REFERENCES
ADD/DROP/MODIFY	CHECK constraints
DROP	Constraints
ADD	UNIQUE constraints
ADD	PRIMARY KEY constraints
MODIFY	Partitioned Primary Indexes
REVALIDATE	Partitioned Primary Indexes

Figure 16.13

Here are two examples:

```
ALTER TABLE emp_job_table, FALLBACK;
ALTER TABLE emp_job_table ADD PRIMARY KEY (job_no, emp_no);


BEFORE:
CREATE SET TABLE CSQL_CLASS.emp_job_table ,NO FALLBACK ,
     NO BEFORE JOURNAL,
     NO AFTER JOURNAL,
     CHECKSUM = DEFAULT
     (
      job_no INTEGER NOT NULL,
      emp_no INTEGER NOT NULL)
PRIMARY INDEX ( job_no );


AFTER:
CREATE SET TABLE CSQL_CLASS.emp_job_table ,FALLBACK ,
     NO BEFORE JOURNAL,
     NO AFTER JOURNAL,
     CHECKSUM = DEFAULT
     (
      job_no INTEGER NOT NULL,
      emp_no INTEGER NOT NULL)
PRIMARY INDEX ( job_no )
UNIQUE INDEX ( job_no ,emp_no );
```

Figure 16.14

When adding a constraint, no other options can be specified. Also notice how the PK became a USI.

Dropping Database Objects

To remove a table, view, or macro from a database, use the DROP command. The general syntax is:

DROP { TABLE | VIEW | MACRO } [*databasename.*] *objectname* ;

Example:

DROP TABLE names_table ;

Figure 16.15

Renaming Database Objects

To change the name of a database object, use the RENAME command. The general syntax is:

RENAME { TABLE | VIEW | MACRO } [databasename.] oldobjectname { TO | AS } [databasename.] newobjectname ;

Example:

RENAME TABLE csql_class.stats_table TO csql_class.mystats_table;

Figure 16.16

Partitioned Tables

Single-level PPI Table

The previous examples have shown NPPI tables, which is the normal way of storing rows. The rows of NPPI table are hash-distributed across the AMPs and sorted by row hash.

When a table or join index is created with a PPI, its rows are hashed to the appropriate AMPs and then assigned to their computed internal partition number based on the value of a partitioning expression defined by the user when the table was created or altered. Once assigned to a partition, the rows are stored in row hash order.

PPI tables provide enhanced storing, deleting, and retrieval of rows when the Parser determines that the PPI can be used instead of a NUSI or a full-table scan.

The following is an example of an SLPPI table creation, based upon the current csql_class.sales_table:

```
CREATE TABLE ppi_sales_table
(product_id INTEGER
,sale_date DATE
,daily_sales DEC(9,2)
)
PRIMARY INDEX (product_id)
PARTITION BY RANGE_N (sale_date BETWEEN DATE '2007-09-01'
AND DATE '2007-10-30'
EACH INTERVAL '1' DAY);

INSERT INTO ppi_sales_table SELECT * FROM sales_table;

COLLECT STATISTICS COLUMN (product_id, sale_date) ON
ppi_sales_table;
```

Figure 16.17

EXPLAIN SELECT * FROM ppi_sales_table
WHERE sale_date = '2007-09-30';


```
Explanation
-----------------------------------------------------------
  1) First, we lock a distinct CSQL_CLASS."pseudo table"
     for read on a RowHash to prevent global deadlock for
     CSQL_CLASS.ppi_sales_table.
  2) Next, we lock CSQL_CLASS.ppi_sales_table for read.
  3) We do an all-AMPs RETRIEVE step from a single
     partition of CSQL_CLASS.ppi_sales_table with a
     condition of ("CSQL_CLASS.ppi_sales_table.sale_date =
     DATE '2007-09-30'") with a residual condition of
     ("CSQL_CLASS.ppi_sales_table.sale_date =
     DATE '2007-09-30'") into Spool 1 (group_amps), which
     is built locally on the AMPs.  The size of Spool 1 is
     estimated with no confidence to be 3 rows (159 bytes).
     The estimated time for this step is 0.02 seconds.
  4) Finally, we send out an END TRANSACTION step to all
     AMPs involved in processing the request.
  -> The contents of Spool 1 are sent back to the user as
     the result of statement 1.  The total estimated time
     is 0.02 seconds.
```

Figure 16.18

To delete the oldest month of rows and create a new partition for a new month, do the following:

```
ALTER TABLE ppi_sales_table
MODIFY PRIMARY INDEX (product_id)
DROP RANGE BETWEEN DATE '2007-09-01' AND DATE '2007-09-30'
EACH INTERVAL '1' DAY
ADD RANGE BETWEEN DATE '2007-11-01' AND DATE '2007-11-30'
EACH INTERVAL '1' DAY
WITH DELETE;
```

Figure 16.19

Note: Altering or dropping a partition can adversely affect performance of queries against the table. A full table scan may result once the partition has been removed, especially when performing range based queries.

Multilevel PPI Tables

Multilevel partitioning allows each partition at a given level to be further partitioned into sub-partitions. Each partition for a level is sub-partitioned the same per a partitioning expression defined for the next lower level. The system hash orders the rows within the lowest partition levels. Teradata combines multiple "where" predicates that result in partition elimination.

The following example shows how an insurance company's claims table could be partitioned by a range of claim dates and then sub-partitioned by a range of state identifiers using multilevel partitioning.

```
CREATE TABLE claims
(claim_id INTEGER NOT NULL
,claim_date DATE NOT NULL
,state_id BYTEINT NOT NULL
,claim_info VARCHAR(20000) NOT NULL
)
PRIMARY INDEX (claim_id)
PARTITION BY (RANGE_N(claim_date BETWEEN DATE '1999-01-01'
AND DATE '2005-12-31' EACH INTERVAL '1' MONTH)
,RANGE_N(state_id BETWEEN 1 AND 75 EACH 1))
UNIQUE INDEX (claim_id);
```

Figure 16.20

Eliminating all but one month out of their many years of claims history would facilitate scanning of less than 5 percent of the claims history for satisfying the following query:

```
SELECT *
FROM claims
WHERE claim_date BETWEEN DATE '2005-06-01'
AND DATE '2005-06-30';
```

Figure 16.21

Similarly, eliminating all but the Connecticut claims from the many states in which this insurance company does business would make it possible to scan less than 5 percent of the claims history to satisfy the following query:

```
SELECT *
FROM claims, states
WHERE claims.state_id = states.state_id
AND states.state = 'Connecticut';
```

Figure 16.22

Combining both of these predicates for partition elimination makes it possible to scan less than 0.5 percent of the claims history to satisfy the following query:

```
SELECT *
FROM claims, states
WHERE claims.state_id = states.state_id
AND states.state = 'Connecticut'
AND claim_date BETWEEN DATE '2005-06-01'
AND DATE '2005-06-30';
```

Figure 16.23

Clearly, combining both predicates for partition elimination has a significant performance advantage. Partition elimination by both of these columns, as described, provides higher performance, more space efficiency, and more maintenance efficiency than a composite NUSI or join index for most of the queries run at this insurance company.

Queue Tables

A queue table is a special database object: a persistent table used to handle queue-oriented data such as event processing, and asynchronous data loading applications. The properties of queue tables are similar to those of ordinary base tables, with the additional unique property of behaving like an asynchronous first-in-first-out (FIFO) queue.

You can think of a queue table as a regular table that also has a memory-resident cache associated with it that tracks the FIFO queue ordering of its rows. Additionally, consumed rows are retrieved and deleted from the database simultaneously, which ensures that no row can be processed more than once.

An ideal queue table has the following characteristics:

- Low cardinality (implying that its rows are consumed at roughly the same rate as they are inserted).
- Infrequent UPDATE operations to its rows.
- Infrequent DELETE operations on its rows.

A queue table might be used to process event alerts.

SYNTAX

CREATE [SET/MULTISET] TABLE *tablename*, QUEUE [, <Create Table Options>]
      (*QITS_column_name* TIMESTAMP(6) NOT NULL
        DEFAULT CURRENT_TIMESTAMP(6)
       [<data_attributes> <constraints>]
     [, <Additional Column Definitions>])
     <Table-level Constraints>
     <Index Definitions>;

The first column defined for any queue table must be a Query Insertion Timestamp (QITS) column. The system uses the QITS column to maintain the FIFO ordering of rows in the queue table. Each queue table has only one QITS column, and it must be defined with the following attributes:

column_name TIMESTAMP(6) NOT NULL DEFAULT CURRENT_TIMESTAMP(6)

The following example illustrates the creation of a Queue table:

```
CREATE TABLE qtbl_5
,QUEUE
(qits TIMESTAMP(6) NOT NULL DEFAULT CURRENT_TIMESTAMP(6)
,qsn INTEGER GENERATED ALWAYS AS IDENTITY (NO CYCLE)
,col_3 INTEGER
)
UNIQUE PRIMARY INDEX (qsn)
INDEX (qits);
```

Figure 16.24

Trigger Processing

Triggers are associated with tables, and can be used to automate required steps whenever an INSERT, UPDATE, or DELETE is performed.

Some possible uses are:
- Business Rules
  - Update the inventory table when a sale is made.
  - Reorder an item when On Hand Quantity falls below a given point.
- Event Propagation
  - Send an email when a new customer is added.

- Summary Table Maintenance
  - o Maintain a summary table if high value items are sold.
  - o Can also use a Join Index to accomplish this.
- Audit Trail
  - o Create a log of changes.
- Data Validation
  - o Rollback bad changes.

TRIGGER Commands

CREATE TRIGGER	Creates a new trigger definition
REPLACE TRIGGER	Changes the definition for a trigger without having to drop and recreate it. If the named trigger does not exist, a new trigger will be created.
DROP TRIGGER	Removes a trigger from the system.
ALTER TRIGGER	This is a Teradata extension. It allows you to change the status of a trigger from DISABLED to ENABLED before/after loading.

Figure 16.25

CREATE / REPLACE TRIGGER Syntax

CREATE TRIGGER creates a new trigger definition.

REPLACE TRIGGER changes the definition for a trigger without having to drop and recreate it.

CREATE | REPLACE TRIGGER *trigger_name*
<trigger status> <trigger action time> <triggering event>
<trigger sequence> <referencing clauses> <trigger type>
<trigger firing condition> <triggered action>

TRIGGER COMPONENTS

Component	Purpose	Choices	
Trigger Status	Can be changed using ALTER TRIGGER	ENABLED DISABLED	
Trigger Action Time	When the trigger action should happen	BEFORE or AFTER the triggering statement is executed	
Triggering Event or Statement	Which action on the subject table causes the trigger to fire.	**Triggering Event**	
		INSERT	Is one of the following: • INSERT • INSERT ... SELECT • Atomic Upsert • MERGE
		DELETE	Is a DELETE
		Triggering Statement	
		UPDATE	Is one of the following: • UPDATE • Atomic Upsert • MERGE Any number of rows, including none, can be updated.

Teradata 12 Certification Study Guide

Trigger Sequence	Allows you to control the order of trigger execution within a request when multiple triggers are defined on a subject table.	ORDER *<value>*
Referencing Clause	The references are to virtual variables and tables, which can include values from the subject table either before or after the data-changing statement.	OLD ROW or OLD TABLE NEW ROW or NEW TABLE
Trigger Type	Causes the triggered action to occur once per statement for a statement trigger and once per row for a row trigger.	STATEMENT ROW
Trigger Firing Condition	Defines the additional conditions that must be met for the triggered action to occur.	e.g. WHEN n.qoh < 5
Triggered Actions	Defines which SQL statement causes the triggered action to occur.	SET, INSERT, UPDATE, DELETE, CALL, ABORT, EXEC

Figure 16.26

Using Triggers Effectively

- Use EXPLAIN
  - o Think about scalability
  - o Try to limit all-AMP operations
- Use statement triggers when the statement that fires the trigger changes a lot of rows
- Consider alternatives to triggers
  - o Use a Join Index to maintain a summary table
  - o Use Referential Integrity to validate changes
  - o May be able to use upsert (UPDATE ... ELSE INSERT ...)
- Be careful with loading
  - o Triggers must be disabled to use MultiLoad
  - o May have performance/locking issues with TPump
- Statement triggers use steps against a set of rows
- Row triggers re-execute steps for each row
- Typically, use row triggers for single-row changes

Using Roles

A role can be viewed as a pseudo-user with privileges on a number of database objects. Any user granted a role can take on the identity of the pseudo-user and access all of the objects it has rights to. A database administrator can create different roles for different job functions and responsibilities, grant specific privileges on database objects to these roles, and then grant these roles to users.

Advantages of roles include:

- Simplify access rights administration
- Reduce disk space usage
- Better performance
- Less dictionary contention during DDL operations because the commands use less time.

Teradata 12 Certification Study Guide

A database administrator can grant rights on database objects to a role and have these rights automatically applied to all users assigned to that role. When a user's function within his organization changes, it is easier to change his/her role than deleting old rights and granting new rights that go along with the new function.

Roles can improve performance and reduces dictionary contention for DDL if they are fully utilized on a Teradata system.

Implementing Roles

Roles define access privileges on database objects. When you assign a default role to a user, you give the user access to all the objects that the role has been granted privileges to. A default role that has a role as a member gives the user additional access to all the objects that the nested role has privileges to. A newly created role does not have any associated privileges until grants are made to it. To manage user access privileges with roles, you can do the following:

- Create different roles for different job functions and responsibilities.

- Grant specific privileges on database objects to the roles.

- Assign default roles to users.

- Add members to the role.

- Members of a role can be users or other roles.

- Roles can only be nested one level. Thus, a role that has a role member cannot also be a member of another role.

Use the CREATE USER / MODIFY USER command to assign a DEFAULT ROLE for a specific user as the following example demonstrates.

Create User CSQL01 AS DEFAULT ROLE = new_role;

Modify User CSQL01 AS DEFAULT ROLE = new_role;

Figure 16.27

Note: A user executing the CREATE USER / MODIFY USER command with the DEFAULT ROLE option must have ADMIN privileges on the specified role (i.e. new_role).

Practice Questions

1. Creating VOLATILE MULTISET tables is not permitted.
   a. TRUE
   b. FALSE

2. A Primary Key definition will override an explicit Primary Index definition.
   a. TRUE
   b. FALSE

3. Which table names are illegal?
   a. mY#tABLE
   b. My$table&view
   c. $12345
   d. 55#table
   e. z
   f. index

4. Multi-column constraints are defined:
   a. After the final column definition.
   b. At the beginning of the column definitions.
   c. After the Primary Index definition.

5. Users must issue additional INSERTs, UPDATEs, and DELETEs to maintain join indexes.
   a. TRUE
   b. FALSE

6. MLPPI tables are created by specifying multiple RANGE_N clauses in a comma-separated list enclosed within a set of parentheses.
   a. TRUE
   b. FALSE

7. A queue table handles rows on a:
   a. LIFO basis.
   b. FIFO basis.
   c. Random basis

8. Every queue table must have Query Insertion Timestamp column as its first column.
   a. TRUE
   b. FALSE

9. Statement triggers re-execute steps for each row.
   a. TRUE
   b. FALSE

Chapter Notes

Utilize this space for notes, key points to remember, diagrams, areas of further study, etc.

Teradata 12 Certification Study Guide

Chapter 17: Temporary Tables

Certification Objectives

- ✓ Given a scenario, identify the type of table that should be used (Global Temporary, Volatile, and Permanent).
- ✓ Identify the functionality of recursive queries.

Before You Begin

You should be familiar with the following terms and concepts.

Terms	Key Concepts
Derived Tables	Non-Recursive and Recursive WITH Statements
Volatile Table	Knowledge on how to apply and options available
Global Temporary	Features vs. Volatile Tables
Uses	General Practices for using temporary tables

There are three types of temporary tables: Derived, Volatile, and Global Temporary tables. The following chart provides a quick overview of the differences between the types of temporary tables. We will discuss each type of temporary table in this chapter.

TEMPORARY TABLE TYPE	DEFINITION
Derived	• Exist only within a query. • Space comes from the user's Spool space.
VOLATILE	• Definition and data exist only within the user's session.

	• It is not recorded in the Data Dictionary. • Space comes from the user's Spool space.
GLOBAL TEMPORARY	• Definition is stored in the Data Dictionary, and can be used by other users. • Data exists only within the user's session. • Space comes from the user's Temporary space.

Figure 17.1

Derived Tables

Derived tables are created, used, and dropped as part of a query. They allow the use of aggregates in a WHERE clause. This query locates all employees whose salary is greater than the company average.

```
SELECT  last_name
       ,salary        (FORMAT '$,$$$,$99.99')
       ,avgsal        (FORMAT '$,$$$,$99.99')
 FROM
        /* Insert this data into the derived table */
        /* The subquery must be enclosed in parentheses */
 (SELECT AVG (salary) FROM employee_table)
        /* Derived tablename and column(s) */
 my_temp (avgsal)
        /* Main query table */
 ,employee_table
 WHERE salary > avgsal
 ORDER BY 2 DESC;


Result: 5 rows returned


Last_name                    Salary          avgsal
--------------------    ------------    ------------
Gere                     $64,300.00      $46,879.93
Strickland               $54,590.00      $46,879.93
Ford                     $54,590.00      $46,879.93
Student                  $48,850.00      $46,879.93
Roberts                  $48,800.00      $46,879.93
```

Figure 17.2

The (SELECT AVG (salary) FROM employee_table) functions as an INSERT INTO followed by the declaration of the derived table's name and column name(s) *my_temp (avgsal).* There must be a one-for-one match between the projected columns in the SELECT and columns in the derived table. The derived table columns take their data type from the projected columns.

Non-Recursive WITH

The Non-Recursive WITH is another way to create and use Derived tables. The main difference is that they are no longer defined in the FROM statement. Instead, they are defined at the beginning of the query as seen in the following syntax:

WITH *named_query* (*columnnames*)
(*select expression(s)*
) <final query to show the results>;

The named query is similar to a derived table.

```
WITH query_name(dept, totalsal) AS
(SELECT dept_no, SUM(salary)
 FROM   employee_table
 GROUP BY dept_no
)
SELECT d.dept_no AS Dept
     , TRIM(department_name) AS DeptName
     , Budget  (FORMAT '$,$$$,$$$.99') AS BudgetAmt
     , TotalSal (FORMAT '$,$$$,$$$.99') AS TotalSalaries
FROM   department_table d
JOIN   query_name
ON     d.dept_no = dept
ORDER BY 1;

Result: 4 rows returned

  Dept  DeptName                  BudgetAmt   TotalSalaries
  ----- ---------------------    -----------  -------------
   100  Marketing                $500,000.00    $48,850.00
   200  Research and Develop     $550,000.00    $91,588.88
   300  Sales                    $650,000.00    $40,200.00
   400  Customer Support         $500,000.00   $144,180.00
```

Figure 17.3

Teradata 12 Certification Study Guide

RECURSIVE WITH

The RECURSIVE WITH is another variation of a Derived table. The major difference is that a set operator is used within the derived table. The recursive nature causes the table to be joined multiple times as long as there are matching rows recursively being generated. The general syntax of a RECURSIVE WITH is:

WITH RECURSIVE *named_query* (*columnnames*)
(<root select statement>
 UNION ALL
 <recursive select statement>
)
<final query to show the results>;

The following example uses the single-table recursion that exists in the employee_table. Employees have managers, and managers are also employees. Knowing that whoever is at the top of the hierarchy does not have a manager (currently) we start there and have the system work its way down.

```
WITH RECURSIVE query_name (employee_no, last_name, depth) AS
( SELECT root.employee_no,  root.last_name, 0 AS depth
FROM employee_table  root
WHERE root.mgr_employee_no IS NULL
UNION ALL
SELECT indirect.employee_no,  indirect.last_name, seed.depth+1 AS
depth
FROM query_name  seed, employee_table  indirect
WHERE seed.employee_no = indirect.mgr_employee_no
AND depth <= 20
)
SELECT employee_no, last_name, depth FROM query_name
ORDER BY depth;
```

```
Result: 9 rows returned

employee_no   last_name                    depth
-----------   --------------------         -----
    1121334   Strickland                     0
    2000000   Travolta                       1
    1000234   Gere                           1
    1333454   Roberts                        1
    1324657   Willis                         2
    2312225   Mcfly                          2
    1256349   Ford                           2
    1232578   Student                        3
    2341218   Clooney                        3
```

Figure 17.4

Teradata 12 Certification Study Guide

Volatile and Global Temporary Tables

Temporary tables are ideal for holding intermediate data to be repeatedly used for queries by the user in their current session. This is a big advantage over derived tables.

Temporary tables are visible only to the user / session that create them. In addition, several users can create the same temporary tables and each user will see only their own version of the table. For example, suppose you need to run several complex queries on large tables during a session. An efficient strategy is to execute the complex query once, then store the result in a temporary table.

SYNTAX

CREATE [SET | MULTISET] [VOLATILE | GLOBAL TEMPORARY] TABLE tablename
, [NO] LOG <other table definitions>
<column definitions>
<index definitions>
ON COMMIT [DELETE | PRESERVE] ROWS

OPTION	DEFINITION
[NO] LOG	The default is to record all INSERT, DELETE, and UPDATE operations. Though this is slower, it makes the table data recoverable in case of a restart. LOG is the default.
ON COMMIT	DELETE ROWS – In Teradata transaction mode, each statement is a transaction, unless it appears within a multi-statement request BT; . . . ET; Therefore, if you were to do an INSERT into a temporary table, the row would be deleted as soon as the INSERT completes. In ANSI transaction mode, the row would remain until a COMMIT is issued.

	DELETE is the default.
	PRESERVE ROWS – Rows will remain until deleted or End of Session.

Figure 17.5

Volatile Tables

Volatile tables do not have a persistent definition; they must be newly created each time you need to use them. The table definition is cached only for the duration of the session in which it is created.

If you frequently reuse particular volatile table definitions, consider writing a macro that contains the CREATE TABLE text for those volatile tables.

Because volatile tables are private to the session that creates them, the system does not check their creation, access, modification, or drop privileges.

The following list details the general characteristics of volatile tables:
- Both the contents and the definition of a volatile table are destroyed when a system reset occurs.
- Space usage is charged to the login user Spool space.
- A single session can materialize up to 1,000 volatile tables at one time.
- The primary index for a volatile table can be either an NPPI or a PPI.
- You cannot create secondary, hash, or join indexes on a volatile table.
- You cannot collect statistics on volatile table columns, including the PARTITION column of a PPI volatile table.

The following options are not permitted for volatile tables:
- Referential integrity constraints
- CHECK constraints
- Permanent journaling
- Compressed column values
- DEFAULT clause
- TITLE clause
- Named indexes

Otherwise, the options for volatile tables are identical to those for global temporary tables.

Below is a step-by-step example of building and utilizing a Temporary Table.

Step 1: Create the Temporary Table

```
CREATE VOLATILE  TABLE  dept_aggr_t
(dept_no      SMALLINT
,sum_salary   DECIMAL(10,2)
,avg_salary   DECIMAL(8,2)
,max_salary   DECIMAL(8,2)
,min_salary   DECIMAL(8,2)
,cnt_salary   INTEGER )
PRIMARY INDEX(dept_No)
ON COMMIT PRESERVE ROWS;
```

Figure 17.6

- You *cannot* collect statistics on a volatile table
- Even though a volatile table exists only within a user's current session, the HELP and SHOW TABLE commands can be used to view information about the table.
- ALTER TABLE cannot be used for VOLATILE tables.

Note: For TD12: Any time the Optimizer requires statistics for a volatile table, it requests an all-AMPs sample to get an estimate of the cardinality of the volatile table. This differs from the standard random AMP sample where the system samples rows from a single AMP only.

Global Temporary Tables

Global Temporary tables have a persistent definition but do not have persistent contents across sessions.

The following list details the general characteristics of global temporary tables:
- Space usage is charged against the temporary space of the user who owns the session.
- A single session can materialize up to 2,000 global temporary tables at one time.
- You materialize a Global Temporary table locally by referencing it in a data manipulation statement. To materialize a global temporary table, you must have the appropriate privilege on the base Global Temporary table or on the containing database or user as required by the statement that materializes the table.
- Any number of different sessions can materialize the same table definition, but the contents are different depending on the DML statements made against the individual materialized tables during the course of a session.
- The primary index for a Global Temporary table can be either an NPPI or a PPI.
- You cannot create a Global Temporary table with the ... AS ... WITH DATA. To use the ... AS ... feature to create a Global Temporary table, specify WITH NO DATA.

The following options are not permitted for global temporary tables:
- Referential integrity constraints

- Permanent journaling
- You cannot create secondary, hash, or join indexes on a Global Temporary table.
- You cannot collect the following types of statistics on Global Temporary tables:
  - Multicolumn statistics
  - PARTITION or PARTITION#Ln statistics
  - Sampled statistics

Access checking is not done on the materialized instances of any Global Temporary tables because those tables exist only for the duration of the session in which they are materialized.

```
CREATE MULTISET GLOBAL TEMPORARY TABLE gtt_report_layout
,FALLBACK
(rpt_c01 INT NOT NULL
,rpt_c02 CHAR(12) NOT NULL
,rpt_c03 CHAR(20)
,rpt_c04 SMALLINT
,rpt_c06 CHAR(15)
,rpt_c07 VARCHAR(40)
) PRIMARY INDEX (rpt_c01);
```

Figure 17.7

To modify a temporary table, use the ALTER command. Keep in mind that the default for Volatile and Temporary table data is ON COMMIT <u>DELETE</u> ROWS. To change that, do the following:

```
ALTER TABLE gtt_report_layout, ON COMMIT PRESERVE ROWS;


SHOW TABLE gtt_report_layout;

CREATE MULTISET GLOBAL TEMPORARY TABLE
CSQL_CLASS.gtt_report_layout
,FALLBACK ,CHECKSUM = DEFAULT,LOG
     (
     rpt_c01  INTEGER NOT NULL,
     rpt_c02  CHAR(12) CHARACTER SET LATIN
             NOT CASESPECIFIC NOT NULL,
     rpt_c03  CHAR(20) CHARACTER SET LATIN
             NOT CASESPECIFIC,
     rpt_c04  SMALLINT,
     rpt_c06  CHAR(15) CHARACTER SET LATIN
             NOT CASESPECIFIC,
     rpt_c07  VARCHAR(40) CHARACTER SET LATIN
             NOT CASESPECIFIC)
PRIMARY INDEX ( rpt_c01 )
ON COMMIT PRESERVE ROWS;
```

Figure 17.8

Collecting Statistics on Global Temporary Tables

There are two aspects of collecting statistics on Global Temporary tables:

- Defining the statistics on the base Global Temporary table
- Collecting statistics on the data in a materialized instance

To define the statistics, do the following:

COLLECT STATISTICS . . . ON gtt_report_layout;

Statistics are collected for an empty table. This is allowed so that when an instance is created, statistics can be re-collected by simply entering COLLECT STATISTICS on the materialized Global Temporary table without having to specify the desired columns and indexes.

To accomplish that, the user would enter:

COLLECT STATISTICS ON TEMPORARY gtt_report_layout;

Figure 17.9

General Comparisons and Practices

The following are comparison and guidelines to consider when determining which type of "temporary" table to use. Most of the criteria are based on the number of users needing access to the data along with the frequency of use.

Comparisons:

VOLATILE TABLE	GLOBAL TEMPORARY TABLE
Logon; Create volatile table; Load private data into the volatile table; Use the data; Logoff;	Logon; Create Global temporary Table; Define collected statistics; Logoff; Now, authorized users can: Logon; Load private data into their materialization of the global temporary table; Collect statistics on their data; Use their data; Logoff;

Figure 17.10

TEMPORARY TABLE TYPE	BENEFITS AND USE
Derived	A special type of temporary table is the derived table. You can specify a derived table in an SQL SELECT statement. A derived table is obtained from one or more other tables as the result of a subquery. The scope of a derived table is only visible to the level of the SELECT statement calling the subquery. Using derived tables avoids having to use the CREATE and DROP TABLE statements for storing retrieved information and assists in coding more sophisticated, complex queries.
VOLATILE	If you need a temporary table for a single use only, you can define a volatile table. The definition of a volatile table resides in memory but does not survive across a system restart. Using volatile tables improves performance even more than using Global Temporary tables because the system does not store the definitions of volatile tables in the Data Dictionary. Privilege checking is not necessary because only the creator can access the volatile table.

GLOBAL TEMPORARY	Global Temporary tables are tables that exist only for the duration of the SQL session in which they are used. The contents of these tables are private to the session, and the system automatically drops the table at the end of the session. The data of a Global Temporary table resides in memory and does not survive across a system restart. However, the system saves the Global Temporary table definition permanently in the Data Dictionary. The saved definition may be shared by multiple users and sessions with each session getting its own instance of the table.

Figure 17.11

Practice Questions

1. Space for a VOLATILE table comes from the user's:
    a. Spool space
    b. Temporary space
    c. Permanent space

2. Space for a GLOBAL TEMPORARY table comes from the user's:
    a. Spool space
    b. Temporary space
    c. Permanent space

3. The WITH clause can be:
    a. Non-Recursive
    b. Recursive
    c. Either

4. In creating a temporary table, the default of the ON COMMIT is
    a. DELETE ROWS
    b. PRESERVE ROWS

5. A PPI or NPPI primary index can be specified for:
    a. VOLATILE tables
    b. GLOBAL TEMPORARY tables

6. Which statement is true?
    a. You can collect statistics on Volatile tables.
    b. You can collect statistics on Global Temporary tables.

7. Derived tables only exist within a query.
    a. TRUE
    b. FALSE

Chapter Notes

Utilize this space for notes, key points to remember, diagrams, areas of further study, etc.

_____

_____

_____

_____

_____

_____

_____

_____

_____

_____

_____

_____

_____

Chapter 18: Stored Procedures

Certification Objectives

- ✓ Identify the functionality of Stored Procedures.
- ✓ Identify conditions when Stored Procedures may be used.
- ✓ Describe the types and uses of Stored Procedure parameters and variables.
- ✓ Describe methods to debug Stored Procedures.

Before You Begin

You should be familiar with the following terms and concepts.

Terms	Key Concepts
SPL	Knowledge of SPL statements such as those used for logic flow control, variable and cursor declaration and exception handling.
External Stored Procedures	Understanding of how they are different than SQL Stored Procedures (SPs).
DML / DDL	Knowledge of these statements and which ones are available for use in Stored Procedures.

An SQL Stored Procedure is a combination of SQL statements and procedural statements called Stored Procedure Language (SPL) statements. It is not necessary for SQL statements to be present – it may consist solely of SPL statements. An External Stored Procedure is written in C, C++ or Java language. It also may contain SQL however it is submitted using the CLIv2, ODBC or JDBC interfaces. The majority of the information in this section concerns SQL Stored Procedures.

A stored procedure is a database object executed on the Teradata Database. Typically, a stored procedure consists of a procedure name, input and output parameters, and a procedure body.

For each stored procedure, the database stores the SPs consisting of the procedure body you write and the corresponding compiled object code. The Data Dictionary tables contain stored procedure parameters and attributes.

A stored procedure provides control and condition handling statements, in addition to input and output parameters and local variables, which make SQL a computationally complete programming language.

Applications based on stored procedures provide the following benefits over equivalent embedded SQL applications:

- Better performance because of greatly reduced network traffic between the client and server.
- Better application maintenance because business rules are encapsulated and enforced on the server.
- Better transaction control.
- Better application security by restricting user access to procedures rather than requiring them to access data tables directly.
- Better application execution because all SQL language statements are embedded in a stored procedure to be executed on the server through one CALL statement.

Nested CALL statements extend performance by combining all transactions and complex queries in the nested procedures into one explicit transaction, and by handling errors internally in the nested procedures.

Stored Procedures allow the combination of both SPL (Stored Procedures Language) and SQL control statements to manage the delivery and execution of the procedure.

CREATE PROCEDURE

A stored procedure is created like all Teradata objects using a CREATE statement. However, it is stored as an executable piece of code. In order for a stored procedure to be executable, it must be compiled as part of the CREATE request. A stored procedure can be created from the following:

- BTEQ utility using the .COMPILE command
- CLIv2 applications, ODBC, JDBC, and Teradata SQL Assistant using the SQL CREATE PROCEDURE or REPLACE PROCEDURE statement.

Once compiled, the Stored Procedure is stored in a user database as an object, and seen as a "P" when using a HELP USER or HELP DATABASE command.

The following is the basic syntax to CREATE a procedure:

```
CREATE PROCEDURE  [<database-name>.]<procedure-name>
 ( [ <parameter-list> ] )  <procedure-body>;
```

Elements in a Procedure Body

A procedure body can contain the following elements:

Stored procedure body of this type ...	Can contain the following ...
Single statement	one SQL statement or control statement, including dynamic SQL. Note: The following elements are not allowed: • Any declaration (local variable, cursor, or condition handler) statement • A cursor statement (OPEN, FETCH, or CLOSE)
Compound statement	• Local variable declarations • Cursor declarations • Condition handler declaration statements • Control statements • DDL, DCL, and DML statements supported by stored procedures, including dynamic SQL

Figure 18.1

Stored Procedural Language (SPL) Statements

The <procedure-body> may contain any or all of the following SPL commands:
- BEGIN / END – Defines scope and functionality of the procedure body
- CALL – Executes a procedure from a procedure
- CASE/ END CASE – Provides simplified IF/THEN/ELSE logic when processing multiple rows from an open cursor

- DECLARE – Optional, establishes local variables or handler routines for use within the procedure
- FOR / END FOR – Executes a statement for each row fetched from a table by the implied cursor
- IF / END IF - Provides for a conditional test of a variable
- ITERATE - Permits logic branching to defined labels within the stored procedure. Functions like a GO TO statement
- LEAVE – Allows for an exit from a loop
- LOOP / END LOOP – Defines the processing logic to repeat unconditionally
- REPEAT / END REPEAT - Repeats the execution of one or more statements until the specified condition evaluates to true
- SET – Assigns a value to a variable or parameter
- WHILE / END WHILE – Repeats the execution of a statement or statement list while a specified condition evaluates to true

BEGIN / END Statements

The BEGIN and END specifications are both required and they define the body of the procedure. All other SPL commands will be contained within the boundaries delineated by these two statements. Again, they are both required and because of the dependency on each other, they are referred to as a compound statement.

The following demonstrates a simple procedure with a single section used to INSERT a row with all null values into the Customer table:

```
CREATE PROCEDURE First_Procedure ( )
BEGIN
   INSERT INTO Customer_table DEFAULT VALUES;
END;
```

Figure 18.2

To execute the procedure:

```
CALL first_procedure( );
```

Figure 18.3

After the execution of the above procedure, the next SELECT returns:

```
SELECT * FROM customer_table;

Result: 6 rows returned

Customer_Number   Customer_name          Phone_number
---------------   --------------------   ------------
       31313131   Acme Designs           555-5564
              ?   ?                      ?
       31323134   ABC Consulting         555-1010
       57896883   XYZ Landscapers        447-7954
       11111111   Best Electronics       559-9987
       87323456   Database Pros          622-1012
```

Figure 18.4

Establishing Variables and Data Values

A stored procedure can be written to provide additional functionality by naming local variables to store and manipulate values. The variables receive their values either by being explicitly assigned internally or passed from the client that calls the procedure. This can be accomplished by doing the following:

- A DECLARE statement is used to establish the variable.
- A SET statement is used to assign a value to a variable within a procedure.

The value may be a literal or an equation. However, before using a variable name, the name and the data type must be defined.

DECLARE Statement to Define Variables

The DECLARE is primarily used to establish a local variable name for use within the stored procedure. The variable is called 'local' because it is local to the compound statement in which it is defined.

Variable Declaration Rules

Variables within the same procedure need to follow the below rules:

- You can only declare local variables within a BEGIN ... END compound statement.
- You can specify any number of local variable declarations in each BEGIN ... END compound statement. Each declaration must end with a semicolon character.
- Within each declaration, you can specify any number of local variables, separated by commas in a list.
- The scope of a local variable is the BEGIN ... END compound statement in which it is declared and all nested compound statements.
- No two variables declared in a compound statement can have the same name.
- A variable name can, however, be reused in any nested compound statement.
- Each local variable declaration consists of the following elements:
    - Local variable name (mandatory)
    - Variable data type (mandatory)
    - Default value for the local variable (optional)

Variable declaration syntax is:

DECLARE *var1* [, *var2* ...] <data_type> [DEFAULT {*literal* | NULL }] ;

An example is:

DECLARE v01, v02, v03 CHAR(5) DEFAULT 'xxxxx' ;

If the three variables have different data types or default values, then declare them individually:

DECLARE v01 INT;
DECLARE v02 SMALLINT DEFAULT 0;
DECLARE v03 CHAR(20) DEFAULT 'No errors';

Additionally, a variable name cannot be any of these reserved Status variable names:

Status Variable	Description
SQLCODE	Its use has been largely superseded by the use of the ANSI variable SQLSTATE. It is implicitly declared within a stored procedure application as SMALLINT.
SQLSTATE	SQLSTATE is a CHAR(5) value divided logically into a two-character class and a three-character subclass. Subclass values can be any numeric or simple uppercase Latin character string. This is declared implicitly within a stored procedure application.

ACTIVITY_COUNT	The ACTIVITY_COUNT status variable returns the number of rows affected by an SQL DML statement in an embedded SQL or stored procedure application. It is declared implicitly within a stored procedure application as DEC(18,0). ACTIVITY_COUNT is a Teradata extension to the ANSI SQL-2003 standard.

Figure 18.5

A successful completion will assign the value of zero to the SQLSTATE and SQLCODE variables. Since SQLSTATE is a CHAR field, it will be '00000' for comparison purposes.

The next procedure defines var1 as a local variable and assigns an initial value using a DEFAULT and then substitutes the value into the WHERE clause of a DELETE:

```
CREATE PROCEDURE Second_Procedure ( )
  BEGIN
    DECLARE var1   INTEGER   DEFAULT 11111111;
      DELETE FROM Customer_table
      WHERE Customer_number = :var1;
  END;
```

Figure 18.6

SET to Assign a Data Value as a Variable

The SET statement is an assignment statement. Once the variable name and data type have been defined, a value needs to be assigned. As seen above, the DEFAULT can establish an initial value. It may retain the initial value throughout the life of the procedure, or may be modified at any time using a SET command.

The following is an alternate Second_Procedure used to SET the value instead of using DEFAULT:

```
CREATE PROCEDURE Second_Procedure ( )
 BEGIN
  DECLARE var1   INTEGER ;
  SET var1 = 11111111 ;
       DELETE FROM Customer_table
WHERE customer_number = :var1;
 END;
```

Figure 18.7

Assigning a Data Value as a Parameter

Like macros, stored procedures may receive information passed from the client software. This ability provides much more flexibility and enhances the power of stored procedures. When using parameters in a stored procedure, the syntax for a parameter list is comprised of three elements: <parameter-usage> <parameter-name> <data-type>

- <parameter-usage> can be one of these:
    - IN   only provides input from the caller (default)
    - OUT   only provides output to the caller
    - INOUT allows both input and output for the caller
- <parameter-name> is any valid Teradata SQL name
- <data-type> is any valid Teradata data type

The following is an alternative to and a better version of Second_Procedure that receives the value from the CALLer and passes the value for var1 instead of using a DECLARE or SET:

```
CREATE PROCEDURE Second_Procedure (IN  var1 INTEGER )
  BEGIN
        DELETE FROM  Customer_table
  WHERE Customer_number = :var1;
  END;
```

Figure 18.8

CALL Statement

The CALL is used to execute a stored procedure. The CALL statement is normally executed either by a client program or interactively by a user. Additionally, a stored procedure is allowed to call another stored procedure.

The following CALL executes the first procedure shown above:

```
CALL First_Procedure ( );
```

Figure 18.9

Since the First_Procedure does not define any parameters, none are passed to it. However, Second_Procedure has evolved to the point of expecting a parameter value at run time to identify the row to delete. The next CALL executes the Second_Procedure and passes the value of 11111111:

```
CALL Second_Procedure(11111111);
```

Figure 18.10

Now, the procedure can be called again and a different row can be deleted using:

CALL Second_Procedure(31313131);

Figure 18.11

Exception Handling

At times, things may happen within stored procedures that are unexpected. The status variables can be a major help in determining what happened. However, at times, the same error handling logic might be needed multiple times within the same procedure. When this is the case, a Handler routine may be written to "handle" the condition. This is an alternative to coding the same IF statements multiple times.

DECLARE HANDLER Statement

The DECLARE is also used to establish a Handler as well as a variable. A Handler is a section of logic that executes automatically based on error conditions that may occur during the execution of a stored procedure. The syntax for DECLARE HANDLER:

DECLARE <handler-type> HANDLER
FOR { <sqlstate-code-list> | <generic-condition-list> }
<handler-action>;

Syntax element ...	Specifies ...
CONTINUE	executes the handler action and passes control to the next statement following the statement that invoked it.
EXIT	Executes the handler action and then implicitly exits the BEGN...END compound statement in

	which the handler is declared. If the procedure contains no other compound statement, the procedure terminates or returns to its caller.
sqlstate-code	the five-character literal SQLSTATE code to be handled. You can specify any number of valid SQLSTATE values in a comma-separated list, but '00000' which represents successful completion of statements, is not allowed. You can specify either a list of SQLSTATE values or a list of generic conditions, but not both.
SQLEXCEPTION SQLWARNING NOT FOUND	generic condition to be handled. You can specify one of these or any combination of the generic conditions in a comma-separated list in a handler declaration. These can be specified in any order, but you cannot repeat any generic condition in the same compound statement.
handler-action	either a single statement or multiple statements enclosed in a compound statement that defines the handler action. The handler action is executed when a particular exception or completion condition is returned to the application. The statement(s) can be any of the following: • SQL DML, DDL, or DCL statements supported by stored procedures. • Control statements, including nested compound statements.

	Declaration (local variable, cursor, or handler) statements are not allowed as a single statement for handler action. These can be submitted from within a compound statement.

Figure 18.12

The next procedure contains two handler routines, the first one is a CONTINUE type and the second is an EXIT:

```
CREATE PROCEDURE Samp_Hdlr ( )
BEGIN
   DECLARE CONTINUE HANDLER
      FOR SQLSTATE '41020', SQLSTATE '52100'
      INSERT INTO My_Err_Tbl
      VALUES (:SQLSTATE, 'Error Handled');
DECLARE EXIT HANDLER
      FOR SQLEXCEPTION
      INSERT INTO My_Err_Tbl (:SQLSTATE, 'Unknown Error');
END;
```

Figure 18.13

DML Statements

These DML statements are allowed in a stored procedure:

INSERT (using UPI or USI)
UPDATE (using UPI or USI)
DELETE (using UPI or USI)
SELECT-INTO (using UPI or USI)
DELETE using cursor (for multiple rows in FOR statement)
UPDATE using cursor (for multiple rows in FOR statement)
SELECT using cursor (for multiple rows in FOR statement)
Nested CALL statements

Figure 18.14

The syntax for the SELECT-INTO is:

{ SELECT | SEL } <column-list> INTO <assignment-target-list>
FROM <table-name>
WHERE <comparison>
[<other-clauses>];

Here's an example:

```
CREATE PROCEDURE NewProc
(IN name CHAR(12),
IN number INTEGER,
IN dept INTEGER,
IN salary DECIMAL(10,2),
OUT dname CHAR(10))
        BEGIN
        INSERT INTO Employee_Table
                (EmpName, EmpNo, DeptNo, Salary_Amount)
                VALUES (:name, :number, :dept, :salary);
        SELECT DeptName INTO dname FROM Department
        WHERE DeptNo = dept;
END;
```

Figure 18.15

DDL Statements

The following DDL statements in a stored procedure are allowed when the creator is also the owner of the procedure. That is, a stored procedure can contain DDL statements only if it is created in the database of the user.

ALTER FUNCTION	CREATE TRIGGER	DROP USER
ALTER TABLE	CREATE USER	DROP VIEW
ALTER TRIGGER	CREATE VIEW	END LOGGING
BEGIN LOGGING	DELETE DATABASE	MODIFY DATABASE
COLLECT STATISTICS (Optimizer Form)	DELETE USER	LOGGING ONLINE ARCHIVE OFF
COLLECT STATISTICS (QCD Form)	DROP CAST	SET QUERY BAND ... FOR TRANSACTION
COMMENT	DROP DATABASE	MODIFY PROFILE
CREATE CAST	DROP ERROR TABLE	MODIFY USER
CREATE DATABASE	DROP HASH INDEX	RENAME MACRO
CREATE ERROR TABLE	DROP INDEX	RENAME PROCEDURE

CREATE FUNCTION	DROP JOIN INDEX	RENAME TABLE
CREATE HASH INDEX	DROP MACRO	RENAME TRIGGER
CREATE INDEX	DROP ORDERING	RENAME VIEW
CREATE JOIN INDEX	DROP PROCEDURE	REPLACE CAST
CREATE MACRO	DROP PROFILE	REPLACE FUNCTION
CREATE ORDERING	DROP ROLE	REPLACE MACRO
CREATE PROFILE	DROP STATISTICS	REPLACE ORDERING
CREATE ROLE	DROP TABLE	REPLACE TRANSFORM
CREATE TABLE	DROP TRANSFORM	REPLACE TRIGGER
CREATE TRANSFORM	DROP TRIGGER	REPLACE VIEW

Figure 18.16

External Stored Procedures

External stored procedures are written in the C, C++, or Java programming language. In addition, they are installed on the database, and are executed similarly to stored procedures.

Usage

Below is a synopsis of the steps you need to follow in order to develop, compile, install, and use external stored procedures:

- When using Java, place the class or classes for the external stored procedure in a JAR file and call the SQLJ.INSTALL_JAR external stored procedure to register the JAR file and its classes with the database.
- Use CREATE PROCEDURE or REPLACE PROCEDURE for external stored procedures to create a database object for the external stored procedure.
- Use GRANT option to grant privileges to users who are authorized to use the external stored procedure.
- Invoke the procedure using the CALL statement.

Executing SQL from External Stored Procedures

To execute SQL within an External Stored Procedure, use the following guidelines:

- C or C++ external stored procedure use CLIv2
- Java external stored procedure use JDBC

Differences between Stored Procedures and External Stored Procedures

Using external stored procedures is very similar to in-database stored procedures, except for the following:

- Invoking an external stored procedure from a client application does not count against nesting limit.
- To install an external stored procedure on a database, you must have the CREATE EXTERNAL PROCEDURE privilege on the database.
- The CREATE PROCEDURE statement for external stored procedures is different from the CREATE PROCEDURE statement for stored procedures.
- In addition to syntax differences, you do not have to use the .COMPILE command as with BTEQ.

Macros or Stored Procedures for Tactical Queries

Macros were once a better choice than stored procedures for simple requests, multi-statement requests (statements executed in parallel), and statements returning multiple rows because performance was almost always better. Stored procedures now support multi-statement requests and result sets, and with their conditional logic, are a better choice than macros for running tactical queries.

Simple Requests

Stored procedures may perform better than macros for simple requests. You can use either macros or stored procedures to run simple requests.

Multi-statement Requests

Both macros and stored procedures support multi-statement requests. Multi-statement request performance for stored procedures is the same, if not better than, macro performance.

Statements Returning Multiple Rows

Stored procedures now support result sets, which means that a stored procedure can now return multiple rows. Macros have no advantage over stored procedures in returning multiple rows.

Differences between Macros and Stored Procedures

The following table summarizes the differences between macros and stored procedures:

MACRO	STORED PROCEDURE
Limited procedural logic.	Sophisticated procedural logic.
Can return multi-row result sets for the same request.	DYNAMIC RESULT SETS allows the stored procedure to return up to 15 result sets.

Multi-statement request parallelizes multiple single row statements.	Multi-statement request using the BEGIN REQUEST – END REQUEST statements parallelizes multiple single row DML statements.
Macro text stored in dictionary.	Stored procedure text stored in user database.
Can EXPLAIN a macro.	Cannot EXPLAIN a stored procedure. Instead must EXPLAIN each individual stored procedure SQL statement individually.
Can be invoked by a trigger.	Can be invoked by a trigger.

Figure 18.17

Teradata 12 Certification Study Guide

Practice Questions

1. External stored procedures can be written in
   a. COBOL
   b. C
   c. C++
   d. Assembler
   e. SQL
   f. Java
   g. Perl
   h. HTML

2. Macros provide more flexibility than Stored Procedures.
   a. TRUE
   b. FALSE

3. Choose the correct answer.
   a. Macros cannot be invoked by a trigger.
   b. Stored procedures cannot be invoked by a trigger.
   c. Both statements are true.
   d. Both statements are false.

4. Updates using NUSIs are allowed in stored procedures.
   a. TRUE
   b. FALSE

5. The status variable SQLSTATE has been deprecated by ANSI.
   a. TRUE
   b. FALSE

6. The status variable SQLCODE has been deprecated by ANSI.
   a. TRUE
   b. FALSE

7. The body of a procedure is defined by:
   a. WHILE / END WHILE
   b. START / END
   c. BEGIN / LEAVE
   d. ITERATE / END ITERATE
   e. BEGIN / END
   f. DO / END DO

Chapter Notes

Utilize this space for notes, key points to remember, diagrams, areas of further study, etc.

_____

_____

_____

_____

_____

_____

_____

_____

_____

_____

_____

_____

_____

_____

Appendix

Answers to the Chapter Practice Questions

CHAPTER 2
1. b
2. c
3. c
4. b
5. b
6. b

CHAPTER 3
1. c
2. a
3. b
4. b
5. a
6. a

CHAPTER 4
1. b
2. a
3. a
4. a
5. b, d
6. e
7. d

CHAPTER 5
1. b
2. a
3. b, c
4. a
5. b
6. b
7. a

CHAPTER 6
1. b
2. a, c
3. b
4. a
5. b

CHAPTER 7
1. a
2. b
3. b
4. a
5. a, b, d
6. d

CHAPTER 8
1. a
2. a
3. b
4. b
5. a
6. a

CHAPTER 9
1. h
2. a
3. b
4. d
5. c
6. b

CHAPTER 10
1. d
2. b
3. b
4. b
5. d
6. a, b
7. d

CHAPTER 11
1. d
2. a
3. b
4. b
5. c
6. b

CHAPTER 12
1. a
2. a
3. b
4. c
5. b
6. d, e

CHAPTER 13
1. c
2. b
3. a, c
4. a
5. d

CHAPTER 14
1. b
2. b
3. a
4. a
5. a
6. c
7. b

CHAPTER 15
1. b
2. b
3. b
4. d
5. c
6. b
7. a
8. a

CHAPTER 16
1. b
2. b
3. b, d, f
4. a
5. b
6. a
7. b
8. a
9. b

CHAPTER 17
1. a
2. b
3. c
4. a
5. a, b
6. b
7. a

CHAPTER 18
1. b, c, f
2. b
3. d
4. b
5. b
6. a
7. e

Index

Q

R

S

T

U

V

View, 42, 213, 214, 215, 217, 231
Volatile, 283, 289, 290, 294, 298

W

WHERE, 10, 19, 20, 21, 22, 23, 24, 25, 27,
28, 29, 30, 33, 34, 35, 66, 67, 81, 92, 93,
94, 95, 96, 97, 109, 110, 113, 114, 116,
129, 130, 131, 132, 133, 134, 160, 161,
167, 168, 183, 187, 192, 196, 197, 207,
208, 214, 216, 217, 239, 240, 241, 267,
269, 270, 284, 285, 288, 309, 310, 311,
315, 316